W9-BFD-143

STUDENT BOOK 1

JACK C. RICHARDS   DAVID BYCINA   SUE BRIOUX ALDCORN

NEW PERSON TO PERSON

COMMUNICATIVE SPEAKING AND LISTENING SKILLS

OXFORD UNIVERSITY PRESS

Oxford University Press

198 Madison Avenue
New York, NY 10016 USA

Great Clarendon Street
Oxford OX2 6DP England

OXFORD is a trademark of
Oxford University Press.

Library of Congress Cataloging-in-Publication Data
Richards, Jack. C.
    New person to person student book : communicative
listening and speaking skills / Jack C. Richards, David Bycina, Sue
Brioux Aldcorn.
        p. cm.
    ISBN 0-19-434678-1 (1)
    1. English language—Textbooks for foreign speakers. 2.
English language—Spoken English—Problems, exercises, etc. 3.
Listening—Problems, exercises, etc. I. Bycina, David. II. Aldcorn,
Sue Brioux. III. Title: New person to person.
PE1122.R49 1995   94-17962
428.2'4—dc20

Copyright © 1995 Oxford University Press

Editorial Manager: Shelagh Speers
Editors: Kathy Sands Boehmer and Paul Phillips
Associate Editor: Robyn Flusser
Senior Designer: Mark C. Kellogg
Senior Art Buyer: Alexandra F. Rockafellar
Production Manager: Abram Hall

Cover design by Mark C. Kellogg.
Cover photography by Brad Guice.

Illustrations and realia by: Kathryn Adams, Sam Day, Matt Foster,
Elissé Jo Goldstein, Magellan Geographix, Karen Minot, Lori Osiecki,
Debra Page-Trim, Rebecca Perry, William Waitzman, Nina Wallace,
and Rose Zgodzinski.

Location photography by: Richard Haynes, Cynthia Hill,
Stephen Ogilvy, and Rhoda Sidney.

Printing (last digit): 10 9 8 7

Printed in Hong Kong.

The publisher wishes to thank the following for their help in
developing this new edition:
Ms. Charlotte Butler, Kanda Gaigo Gakuin, Tokyo; Ms. Toshiko Oi,
Kokusai Gaigo Senmon Gakko, Osaka; Mr. John Edwards, Sophia
University Community College, Tokyo; Mr. Phillip (PJ) McManus,
Sophia University Community College, Tokyo; Mr. Bill Roberson, Aichi
Kyoiku Daigaku (Aichi University of Education), Nagoya; Ms. Kim
Fine, Sumitomo Electric Industries, Osaka; Mr. Sean McGovern,
Setsunan University, Osaka; Mr. Kenneth Crown, Tokyo Foreign
Language College, Tokyo; Mr. Rory S. Baskin, Koriyama Women's
College, Koriyama; Mr. David Clay Dycus, Aichi Shukutoku Junior
College, Nagoya; Mr. Steve Mierzejewski, Richard Scruggs, and Bob
Mercier, IIST, Fujinomiya; Catherine O'Keefe, OUP, Tokyo.

Sue Brioux Aldcorn wishes to thank the late Dr. Carlos A. Yorio, Four
Seasons Language School, the University of Toronto ESL Program,
and her husband, Skip. Special thanks to Shelagh Speers of Oxford
University Press and Kathy Sands Boehmer for their suggestions,
editorial expertise, and patience.

The publisher also wishes to thank United Artists Pictures, a division
of Metro Goldwyn Mayer, Incorporated and Archive Photos for their
permission to reproduce authentic movie posters.

TO THE STUDENT

Up to now, your study of English has probably focused on the study of English grammar and vocabulary. You already know quite a lot about what the rules of English grammar are, and how to form sentences in English. This knowledge provides an important foundation for you, but it is not enough to enable you to speak English fluently. In order to develop conversational listening and speaking skills, you need practice in these skills, and this is what *New Person to Person* aims to give you.

The focus of each unit in *New Person to Person* is not grammar. Instead, each unit focuses on conversational tasks or functions such as introducing yourself, talking about likes and dislikes, inviting someone to go somewhere, and so on. In order to take part in English conversations, it is necessary to learn how these and other common functions are used in English.

New Person to Person gives you opportunities to listen to native speakers. It also gives you guided practice in using many conversational functions. This is done in the following way:

CONVERSATIONS

Every unit has two sections. Each section begins with a conversation that includes examples of the functions you will be studying in that section. Listen to them on the cassette or as your teacher reads them. You can use them to improve your understanding of spoken English and to hear the language used in both business and social situations.

GIVE IT A TRY

Each function that you hear in the conversation is presented separately. You will be able to concentrate on each one and practice it with a partner until you feel comfortable with it. You will also learn different ways to say the same thing and have the chance to practice using your own ideas.

LISTEN TO THIS

Both sections in each unit end with the opportunity for you to use what you have learned. You will hear conversations that will help you with real-life listening tasks such as finding out opening and closing times, getting directions, and listening to and writing down information on forms.

PERSON TO PERSON

At the end of each unit, you and your partner will work together to solve a problem based on the functions you have just learned. Each of you will have information that the other needs, so you will have to listen to and speak to each other carefully, often using ideas and opinions of your own.

We hope you will find that learning to speak and understand English is easier than you think. Like any skill, it involves practice. *New Person to Person* will guide you through various types of practice, moving from controlled to free use of the language. You can review what you have learned both within each unit and in special review units. The Let's Talk and Review Units at the end of the book provide you with the opportunity to use both the language and your imagination.

Because you will usually work with a partner, *New Person to Person* gives you as much conversational practice as is possible in a classroom situation. Remember, as you practice, that communication is more than just words: People "say" a lot with their faces, their bodies, and their tone of voice.

As you practice with your partner, don't keep your eyes "glued to the book." Instead, use the "read and look up" technique: Look at your line before you speak. Then immediately look at your partner, make eye contact, and say the line as if you were acting. You may look down at your lines as often as you need to, but look at your partner when you speak. This will improve your fluency.

In addition to the language presented in each unit, here are some expressions that will be very useful to you—both in and outside of class.

a. Please say that again.	e. What does _____ mean?
b. I'm sorry. I don't understand.	f. I don't know.
c. Please speak more slowly.	g. May I ask a question?
d. How do you say _____ in English?	h. How do you spell _____?

The speaking and listening practice you get in this book will give you a firm basis for using English outside the classroom and when talking to other speakers of English person to person.

CONTENTS

This is a barbecue.
What happens at barbecues?

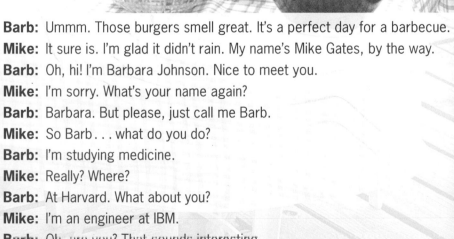

Barb: Ummm. Those burgers smell great. It's a perfect day for a barbecue.

Mike: It sure is. I'm glad it didn't rain. My name's Mike Gates, by the way.

Barb: Oh, hi! I'm Barbara Johnson. Nice to meet you.

Mike: I'm sorry. What's your name again?

Barb: Barbara. But please, just call me Barb.

Mike: So Barb . . . what do you do?

Barb: I'm studying medicine.

Mike: Really? Where?

Barb: At Harvard. What about you?

Mike: I'm an engineer at IBM.

Barb: Oh, are you? That sounds interesting.

Mike: Yeah. I like it. Hey, it looks like the food is ready.

Barb: Good. I'm starving.

1. INTRODUCING YOURSELF

✦ My name's | Mike Gates.
I'm

✧ Hello. | My name's | Barb Johnson.
Hi. | I'm

Introduce yourself to your classmates.

2. GETTING THE NAME RIGHT

Notice how you can ask for and get clarification.

✦ Sorry, what's your *first* name again?
I didn't | catch your | *first* | name.
| get | *last* |

✧ It's | *Barbara*, but please call me *Barb*.
| *Gates, Mike Gates*.

Introduce yourself to other classmates. This time ask the person to repeat his/her first, last, or full name.

3. ASKING SOMEONE'S OCCUPATION

✦ What do you do?

Oh, are you?

✧ I'm | a student.
| a computer analyst.
| an engineer.

✧ How | about you?
What |

Oh, do you?

✦ I work | for Citibank.
| in an office.
| for a trading company.

Ask your partner for his/her occupation. Ask other classmates.

4. ASKING FOR MORE INFORMATION

◆ What do you do?

◇ I'm a student.

◆ Really? What school
do you go to ?

◇ (I go to) | *Boston College.*
| *Seneca College.*

◆ What are you studying?

◇ (I study) | *Business.*
(I'm in) | *Engineering.*
| *Nursing.*

◇ What do you do?

◆ I'm *an engineer.*

◇ Really? What company
do you work for?

◆ I work for | *Suzuki.*
| *a steel company.*

◇ What do you do there exactly?

◆ I'm | *a secretary.*
| in *Human Resources.*
| in *sales.*

Practice

Interview your partner and find out what he/she does. Use one of the models above.

LISTEN TO THIS

▭ Listen to these conversations and complete the information below.

Conversation 1

Man's name:...........................Bradley   Woman's name: ....Owens
Occupation: ....   Occupation: ....

Conversation 2

Woman's name:.........................Jackson   Man's name: ....Hunt
She studies:...............................   He studies:...............................
She goes to:...............................   He goes to:...............................

Conversation 3

Man's name:...............................Pirelli   Woman's name: ....Yamada
His company: ....   Her company:...............................

Where are the people?
What does the woman want to do?

Pronunciation Focus

In compound nouns, the first noun has heavier stress and a higher pitch. Listen and repeat.

SAVINGS account   TELEPHONE number
ZIP code   LAB assistant

Now practice the conversation.
Pay attention to compound nouns.

Officer:	Yes, can I help you?
Ms. Paine:	I'd like to open a savings account.
Officer:	Certainly. First we'll have to fill out a few forms. Could I have your name, please?
Ms. Paine:	It's Paine, Sarah Paine.
Officer:	And how do you spell your last name?
Ms. Paine:	It's P-A-I-N-E.
Officer:	Thank you. Next, is it Miss, Mrs., or Ms.?
Ms. Paine:	I prefer Ms.
Officer:	Fine. Now, could I please have your address, Ms. Paine?
Ms. Paine:	2418 Greystone Road.
Officer:	Is that in Chicago?
Ms. Paine:	Yes, that's right. The zip code is 60602.
Officer:	OK, and please give me your telephone number.
Ms. Paine:	It's 364-9758.
Officer:	364-9758. All right. And finally, Ms. Paine, what is your occupation?
Ms. Paine:	I work at City Hospital. I'm a lab assistant.
Officer:	Fine. I just need some ID, and we'll be all set.

1. NAMES

◆ Could I have your name, please?

◇ It's *Paine. Sarah Paine.*
And how do you spell your | *last* | name?
| *first* |

◆ It's *P-A-I-N-E.*
It's *S-A-R-A-H.*

Practice 1

Role-play with your partner. You are a bank officer. Ask your partner his/her name and how to spell it.

Practice 2

Do the same with three other classmates.

2. ADDRESSES

◆ Where do you live?
Could I have your address?

◇ I live at *2418 Greystone Road.*

◆ Is that in *Chicago?*

◇ Yes, that's right.
No, it's in *River Grove.*

Practice 1

Ask your partner the name of his/her street and how to spell it. Confirm the city.

Practice 2

Ask other classmates.

3. TELEPHONE NUMBERS

| What's your | telephone number? |
| Could I have your | |

(It's) *364-9758.*

Practice 1

Ask your partner his/her telephone number. Repeat it and write it down.

Practice 2

Ask other classmates their names and telephone numbers. Make a list.

Role-play with your partner. Call the operator and ask for the number of one of the people on the list below. (All of them live in Toronto.) Write down the number he/she gives you. Then reverse roles. Now you are the operator and your partner calls you. Use the conversation below as a model.

Operator: Directory Assistance. What city, please?

Caller: Toronto. I'd like the number of Ms. Amanda Rhodes.

Operator: How do you spell the last name, please?

Caller: It's R-H-O-D-E-S.

Operator: Thank you. And could I have the address?

Caller: It's 418 Kingston Road.

Operator: The number is 987-0248.

Caller: 987-0248. Thank you very much.

Operator: You're welcome.

CALLER	**OPERATOR**
Look at this side only.	Look at this side only.

CALLER
Look at this side only.

NAME *Debbie Abel*
ADDRESS *9 Woodgate Rd*
PHONE NUMBER

NAME *Kate Bingham*
ADDRESS *784 Kingston Rd.*
PHONE NUMBER

NAME *Carolyn Bryans*
ADDRESS *12 Lakeside Place*
PHONE NUMBER

NAME *Carl Watson*
ADDRESS *1989 River St.*
PHONE NUMBER

OPERATOR
Look at this side only.

Abel, David, 724 Eastern Ave		867-5307
Abel, Debbie, 9 Woodgate Rd		455-4433
Bingham, Kate, 784 Kingston Rd		767-1690
Bingham, Sue, 621 Landmark Dr		321-5090
Bryans, Carolyn, 12 Lakeside Place		896-3427
Moore, Alex, 845 Cherry St		211-3952
Watson, Carl, 1989 River St		227-5486
Watson, Robert, 18 Palmgrove Blvd		987-2718

LISTEN TO THIS

Listen to the conversation. Fill in the form.

DARCY'S
DEPARTMENT STORE

CREDIT CARD APPLICATION FORM

NAME	TELEPHONE
ADDRESS	
CITY	**STATE** MA **ZIP CODE**
OCCUPATION	**EMPLOYER**
BANK	

PERSON TO PERSON

STUDENT A

(Student A looks at this page. Student B looks at the next page.)

🔊 A tourist is about to go through Customs and Immigration in New York City. You will hear an immigration officer interviewing him.

Practice 1

Listen as the immigration officer helps the tourist. Fill out the form below as you listen.

DISEMBARKATION CARD — U.S. Customs

Surname: ⊔⊔⊔⊔⊔⊔⊔⊔⊔⊔⊔⊔⊔⊔⊔⊔⊔⊔⊔⊔⊔⊔⊔⊔⊔⊔
First name: ⊔⊔⊔⊔⊔⊔⊔⊔⊔⊔⊔⊔⊔⊔⊔⊔⊔⊔⊔⊔⊔⊔⊔⊔⊔⊔
Date of Birth: _____ Day / Month / Year _____
Place of Birth: _____
Nationality: _____
Occupation: _____
Reason for travel in the U.S.: _____
Address in the U.S.: _____

Compare your answers with your partner's.

Practice 2

You have just landed in San Francisco. Your partner is an immigration officer who is going to interview you. Role-play the part of the person below and answer the questions.

This is Ms. Yu-Fen Chan. She was born in Taipei, Taiwan, on September 10, 1951. She is a homemaker visiting her sister. Her sister lives at 63 Carpenter Street in San Francisco.

Practice 3

Now you are the immigration officer. Interview your partner and fill out the disembarkation card below.

DISEMBARKATION CARD — U.S. Customs

Surname: ⊔⊔⊔⊔⊔⊔⊔⊔⊔⊔⊔⊔⊔⊔⊔⊔⊔⊔⊔⊔⊔⊔⊔⊔⊔⊔
First name: ⊔⊔⊔⊔⊔⊔⊔⊔⊔⊔⊔⊔⊔⊔⊔⊔⊔⊔⊔⊔⊔⊔⊔⊔⊔⊔
Date of Birth: _____ Day / Month / Year _____
Place of Birth: _____
Nationality: _____
Occupation: _____
Reason for travel in the U.S.: _____
Address in the U.S.: _____

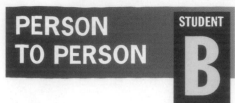
(Student B looks at this page. Student A looks at the previous page.)

🔲 A tourist is about to go through Customs and Immigration in New York City. You will hear an immigration officer interviewing him.

Practice 1

Listen as the immigration officer helps the tourist. Fill out the form below as you listen.

DISEMBARKATION CARD U.S. Customs

Surname: ⌞⌞⌞⌞⌞⌞⌞⌞⌞⌞⌞⌞⌞⌞⌞⌞⌞⌞⌞⌞⌞⌞⌞⌞⌞⌞
First name: ⌞⌞⌞⌞⌞⌞⌞⌞⌞⌞⌞⌞⌞⌞
Date of Birth: _____ / _____ / _____
　　　　　　　　Day　　Month　　Year
Place of Birth: _____
Nationality: _____
Occupation: _____
Reason for travel in the U.S.: _____

Address in the U.S.: _____

Compare your answers with your partner's.

Practice 2

You are a customs officer at the San Francisco airport. Your partner is a tourist who is waiting to clear customs. As you interview him/her, fill out the disembarkation card below.

DISEMBARKATION CARD U.S. Customs

Surname: ⌞⌞⌞⌞⌞⌞⌞⌞⌞⌞⌞⌞⌞⌞⌞⌞⌞⌞⌞⌞⌞⌞⌞⌞⌞⌞⌞
First name: ⌞⌞⌞⌞⌞⌞⌞⌞⌞⌞⌞⌞⌞⌞
Date of Birth: _____ / _____ / _____
　　　　　　　　Day　　Month　　Year
Place of Birth: _____
Nationality: _____
Occupation: _____
Reason for travel in the U.S.: _____

Address in the U.S.: _____

Practice 3

Now you are the tourist and your partner is the immigration officer. Role-play the part of the person below and answer the questions.

This is Jack Harrington. He was born in Sydney, Australia, on April 26, 1947. He is a banker on a business trip, and he is staying at the Sheraton Hotel.

How big is your family?
What family members usually live together?
What do you consider a big family?

Announcer: National Flight 294 to Miami is delayed due to severe weather conditions. Please stand by for additional information.

Maria: Oh no! I hate these long delays!

Jim: I know. I can't wait to get home. I've been on a business trip for a month. I really miss my family.

Maria: A month is a long time to be away. Do you have any children?

Jim: I have three. Two boys and a girl. Would you like to see a picture?

Maria: Oh, how nice! Now, who's this?

Jim: This is Judy, my oldest. She's twenty-four.

Maria: Is she married?

Jim: Yes, she is. And these are my two sons, Jamie and Julian.

Maria: How old are they?

Jim: Jamie is twenty-one. He's in college now. Julian is seventeen, and that's my wife, Beth, next to my daughter.

Maria: Well, you certainly have a lovely-looking family.

Jim: Thank you. So, tell me about your family.

Maria: My husband and I have a son, Tim.

GIVE IT A TRY

1. DESCRIBING YOUR FAMILY

✦ Tell me about your family. Do you have / Have you got | any brothers or sisters? ✧ I have / I've got | *a brother* | but *no sisters.* / and *a sister.* I live with *my parents and my grandparents.* I'm *an only child.*	*grandmother* *grandfather* *mother* *father* *daughter* *son* *aunt* *uncle* *niece* *nephew* *cousin*

Practice 1

Ask your partner if he/she has any brothers or sisters. Your partner will ask you. Then, ask another classmate.

Practice 2

Student A: You are Amy. Answer your partner's questions about your family. Then reverse roles.
Student B: Your partner is Amy. Ask questions about her family. Then reverse roles.

Practice 3

Now, quickly draw your family tree. Tell your partner who the people are. Your partner will tell you about his/her family.

2. DESCRIBING MARITAL STATUS

✦ Are you / Is he/she | married?	✧ Yes, | I am. / he/she is.	✧ No, | I'm not. / he/she isn't. I'm / He/she's | *single.* / *separated.* / *divorced.* / *widowed.*

Practice 1

Ask your classmates if they are married. If everyone is single, choose a marital status.

Practice 2

Ask your partner about the members of Amy's family. Then reverse roles.

3. TALKING ABOUT YOUR CHILDREN

✦ Do you have | any children?
Have you got |

✧ No, I don't.
(Yes.) I have | *three children, two boys and a girl.*
I've got | *a daughter.*

✦ How old | are they?
| is *she?*

✧ *The oldest is twenty-four. The second oldest is twenty-one,
and the youngest is seventeen.*
My son is three and my daughter is six months old.

Practice

Try the conversation above with a partner. Talk about the pictures or your own family.

LISTEN TO THIS

Ellen is showing her friend some pictures from her 50th birthday party.
Number the pictures 1-4 as she talks about each one.

Now listen again and answer these questions.

1. How many children does Ellen have? ....
2. Does she have any grandsons? .... granddaughters? ....
3. How old is her nephew? ....
   How old are her nieces? ....
   What do they do? ....

You can't find your friend.
What do you describe first? Height? Hair? Clothes?

Clerk 1: Oh, darn. Where are they?

Clerk 2: Who?

Clerk 1: I went to get this CD for a woman and her husband. Now I can't find them.

Clerk 2: What do they look like?

Clerk 1: Well, she's fairly tall with curly red hair. He's tall with short blond hair. They look like they're in their late thirties.

Clerk 2: Hmm. I don't see anyone like that. What are they wearing? Do you remember?

Clerk 1: Yeah. He's wearing a red sweatshirt and blue jeans. She's wearing a white skirt and a purple sweater.

Clerk 2: A white skirt and a purple sweater? Hey, wait! I think I see them in the classical section.

Clerk 1: You're right. . . . Sir! Madam! I have that CD you're looking for.

Pronunciation Focus

In normal speech, words like *to, and, are,* and *do* are unstressed and the vowel is reduced to [ə]. Listen.

Word	Reduced pronunciation
to	want to get
and	woman and her husband
are	What are they wearing?
do	What do they look like?
them	I see them over there.

Now practice the conversation. Pay attention to the unstressed words.

1. ASKING ABOUT AGE

| ✦ How old is | he? |
| | she? |

✧ Pretty	young.	He's in his	(mid-) teens.
Fairly	old.	She's in her	(early) seventies.
Kind of			(late) forties.

Practice

Think of three famous people, for example an actor, a singer, an athlete, or a politician. Ask your partner the ages of these people. Use this model:

A: How old is ....?
B: He/she's pretty old/young. (In his/her)....................., I think.

2. ASKING FOR A DESCRIPTION

✦ What does	he	look like?		✧ He's	fairly	tall/short.
	she			She's	pretty	thin/heavy.
					kind of	tall and thin.

What color is	his	hair?		It's	blond.
	her				black.
					gray.

				He	has	brown	hair.
				She		red	
						white	

| What's | his | hair like? | | It's | long/short/medium length. |
| | her | | | | straight/wavy/curly. |

Practice

Look at Amy's family on page 10 again. Describe one of them to your partner. Your partner will guess who you are describing.

Example:
Student A: She has shoulder-length, straight blond hair.
Student B: That's Barbara.

3. DESCRIBING PEOPLE

✦ What is he/she wearing?

◇ He's wearing | *jeans and a red sweatshirt.*
| *a blue suit.*
| *black pants and a green sport shirt.*

She's wearing | *a white skirt and a purple blouse.*
| *a tan uniform.*
| *a pink summer dress.*

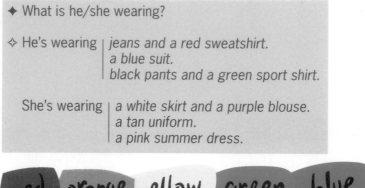

red   orange   yellow   green   blue   purple

pink   gray   black   white   brown   tan

✦ What does he/she have on?

◇ He | has | *a brown jacket* on.
She | | *a yellow hat* on.
| | *a red raincoat* on.
| | *pink shorts and a white T-shirt* on.

Practice

Choose one of the people below. Describe his/her clothing to your partner. Take turns.

LISTEN TO THIS

🔲 Three people all say they witnessed the same crime. Listen as they describe the suspect to a police detective. Fill in the chart below.

	Height	Weight	Age	Hair	Clothing
Witness 1					
Witness 2					
Witness 3					

Look at the chart. What do *you* think the suspect looked like?

PERSON TO PERSON

(Student A looks at this page. Student B looks at the next page.)

Practice 1

Your partner is going to the airport to pick up three friends of yours. Your partner will ask you for their descriptions. Answer his/her questions, but don't give any extra information.
Ask your partner to pick up Angela, Nadine, and Miki.

Example:
Student A: Could you pick up Angela at the airport?
Student B: Sure. What does she look like?

Continue answering questions until your partner can identify the person.

Practice 2

Now, you are going to the airport to pick up three friends for your partner. Ask questions until you can identify each person. Write the name under the correct picture.

(Student B looks at this page. Student A looks at the previous page.)

Practice 1

You are going to the airport to pick up three friends for your partner. Ask your partner for their descriptions. He/she will answer your questions, but will not give you any extra information.

Example:
Student A: Could you pick up Angela at the airport?
Student B: Sure. What does she look like?

Continue asking questions until you can identify each person. Write the name under the correct picture.

Practice 2

Now, ask your partner to pick up Andy, Greg, and Ian. Answer his/her questions.

Who are these people?
What is the man doing?
Do men in your culture like to cook?

Michelle: What are you doing?

Dominic: I'm cooking dinner tonight.

Michelle: That's great. Thank you. What are you making?

Dominic: A surprise. By the way, where do we keep the olive oil?

Michelle: It's in the cabinet over the sink.

Dominic: In the cabinet over the . . . I've got it. Thanks. And . . . do you know where the big pot is?

Michelle: It's in the drawer under the oven.

Dominic: OK. I'm ready. Now, what time do you want to eat?

Michelle: Whenever it's ready, but what can I do to help?

Dominic: Just stay out of the kitchen!

1. ASKING WHERE THINGS ARE

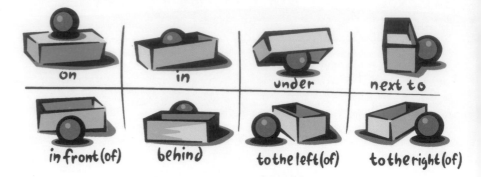

on | in | under | next to

in front (of) | behind | to the left (of) | to the right (of)

✦ Where | is | the *sugar bowl*?
| are | the *coffee cups*?

✧ It's | on the *kitchen table*.
They're | in the *cabinet to the left of the refrigerator*.

Practice 1

You are at a friend's house helping to make dinner. You don't know where anything is. Ask your partner about five of the following things. Then reverse roles. The answers are in the picture.

blender	mugs	plates
toaster	glasses	silverware
coffee maker	cooking pots	sugar
kettle	cups and saucers	rice

Practice 2

Now ask about objects in the classroom.

2. ASKING WHERE THINGS ARE – MORE POLITELY

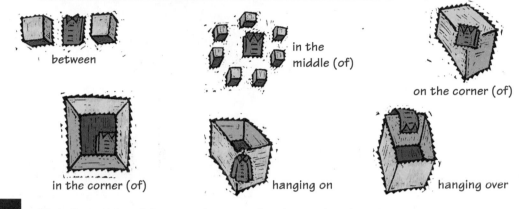

◆ Do you know where my | *suitcase* is?
| *jeans* are?

◇ It's | *in the corner between the dresser and the wall.*
They're | *hanging over the back of the chair.*

between

in the middle (of)

on the corner (of)

in the corner (of)

hanging on

hanging over

Practice

Michelle and Dominic are going away for the weekend.

Student A: You are Dominic. Ask Michelle where the following things are:
your watch, sandals, and *pajamas.*
Student B: You are Michelle. Ask Dominic where the following things are:
your purse, necklace, and *sunhat.*

Take turns. Continue asking about other items.

LISTEN TO THIS

▭ Listen to the four short conversations and answer the following two questions for each.

1. What is the speaker looking for?
a) ....
b) ....
c) ....
d) ....

2. Where is the thing he/she is looking for?
a) ....
b) ....
c) ....
d) ....

Where is this man?

What do you think is wrong?

Do you ever forget the name of an object?

What do you say?

Pronunciation Focus

Notice how final consonants are linked to words beginning with a vowel sound.

come on   the tip of my tongue

does it   color is

Find other linked consonants like this in the conversation and mark them. Then practice the conversation. Pay attention to linked sounds.

Luis: Teresa? . . . I can't find the what-do-you-call-it.

Teresa: What can't you find?

Luis: You know. The thing.

Teresa: What thing?

Luis: Oh, come on . . . you know! It's on the tip of my tongue.

Teresa: What does it look like? Maybe I can help you find it.

Luis: It's a long, narrow, flat thing. It's made of plastic.

Teresa: OK. What color is it, and what's it used for?

Luis: It's red. You use it for drawing straight lines.

Teresa: Luis! You mean the ruler! It's in the box behind the telephone.

Luis: Oh, yeah. I knew that all along. I was just testing you.

1. DESCRIBING THINGS (1)

✦ What size is it?	✧ It's	big/small. long/short. narrow/wide.
✦ What shape is it?	✧ It's	round/a circle. square/a square. rectangular/a rectangle. triangular/a triangle. oval/an oval. flat.
✦ What does it look like?	✧ It's a long, narrow, flat thing.	

Practice

Choose one of the boxes below. Describe it to your partner. Your partner will guess which one you are describing.

Example:
Student A: There is a big, red, round ball. There is a small, blue triangle in front of the ball.
Student B: It's number 1.

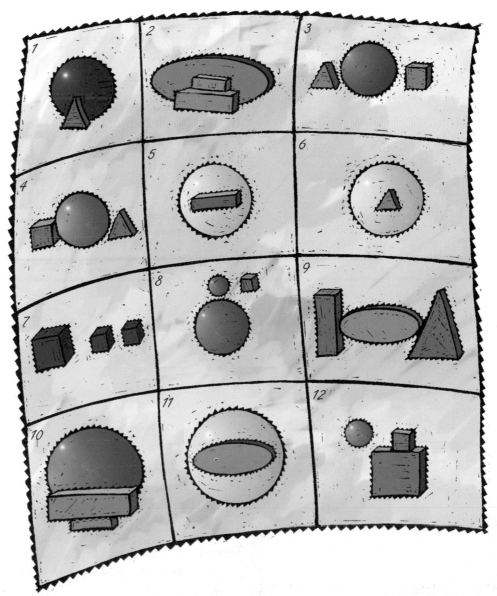

2. DESCRIBING THINGS (2)

✦ What's it What are they	made of?	✧ It's They're	made of	*wood.* *metal.*

Practice

You and your partner have ten minutes to think of as many objects as you can. Write them down and compare your lists with your classmates.

Objects made of
wood:..
plastic:...
metal: ....
cloth:..
glass: ....
paper:...
leather: ....

3. DESCRIBING USES

✦ What	is it are they	used for?	✧ A *knife* is *Scissors* are	used for *cutting.*

Practice

Choose two of the objects below and describe them for your partner to identify. Then reverse roles.

Example:
A: It's long and narrow and it's made of metal.
B: What's it used for?
A: It's used for cutting.
B: It's a knife.

LISTEN TO THIS

 A group of people from long ago are describing their inventions to each other. Listen to the description, and name the object each speaker invented.

Speaker 1	Speaker 5 ....
Speaker 2	Speaker 6 ....
Speaker 3	Speaker 7 ....
Speaker 4	Speaker 8 ....

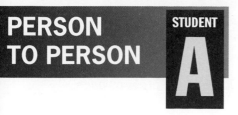

PERSON TO PERSON

STUDENT A

(Student A looks at this page. Student B looks at the next page.)

Bruce and Ron are two American students who are entering their second year of college. They decided to rent an apartment this year instead of living in a college dormitory.

Practice 1

Listen to the conversation and check (✔) the items that Bruce will bring to the apartment.

Practice 2

Briefly describe the items that Bruce is bringing to the apartment. Your partner will describe the items that Ron is bringing. Together, decide where these things will be put in the room. Draw them in the room below.

Practice 3

Compare your room with your partner's. Do they look the same? What's different?

PERSON TO PERSON

STUDENT B

(Student B looks at this page. Student A looks at the previous page.)

Bruce and Ron are two American students who are entering their second year of college. They decided to rent an apartment this year instead of living in a college dormitory.

Practice 1

Listen to the conversation and check (✔) the items that Ron will bring to the apartment.

Practice 2

Briefly describe the items that Ron is bringing to the apartment. Your partner will describe the items that Bruce is bringing. Together, decide where these things will be put in the room. Draw them in the room below.

Practice 3

Compare your room with your partner's. Do they look the same? What's different?

What do you do on your birthday?

Karen: Greg, when is Sheila's birthday? Is it this week?

Greg: Yeah, it's this Saturday, the twenty-eighth.

Karen: I'd really like to see her on her birthday. Are you two doing anything?

Greg: Well, yes, we have tickets to a concert at Carnegie Hall.

Karen: What time does it start?

Greg: It starts at 8:00.

Karen: Hmmm... I'm afraid I can't make it by then. I have to work late on Saturday. Hold on... I have an idea. What time does the concert end?

Greg: Pretty late. Probably around half-past eleven.

Karen: Well, how about going to the Cafe Alfredo for some coffee and birthday cake after the concert? I'll meet you there.

Greg: Well, what time does the cafe close?

Karen: It's open until at least 1:00. Come on, admit it... it's a fabulous idea.

Greg: OK, OK, Karen. We'll see you then!

1. DAYS AND DATES

✦ When	is your *birthday*?		✧ It's *on*	Monday.
	is your *anniversary*?			October 13.
	is the *party*?			
			It's *in*	October.

Find out when your classmates' birthdays are. Do any of your classmates share the same birthday?

2. STARTING AND FINISHING TIMES

✦ When	does the *concert*	start?	✧ It	starts *at 8:00 (sharp)*.
What time		end?		ends *about 10:15*.

Student A
Ask your partner when three of the following events start and finish: movie, concert, opera, ballet, baseball game. Then reverse roles. Your partner will ask you about three events. Use this conversation as a model:

A: What time does the....................start?

B: ....

A: And when does it end?

B: ....

Student B
Use the entertainment guide below to find the starting times. Ending times are two hours later for the movie and concert; three hours later for the opera, ballet, and baseball game. Use this conversation as a model:

A: ....?

B: At eight o'clock (sharp).

A: ....?

B: At about ten.

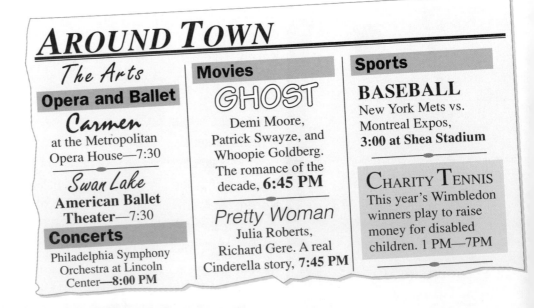

AROUND TOWN

The Arts

Opera and Ballet

Carmen
at the Metropolitan
Opera House—7:30

Swan Lake
**American Ballet
Theater**—7:30

Concerts

Philadelphia Symphony
Orchestra at Lincoln
Center—**8:00 PM**

Movies

GHOST
Demi Moore,
Patrick Swayze, and
Whoopie Goldberg.
The romance of the
decade, **6:45 PM**

Pretty Woman
Julia Roberts,
Richard Gere. A real
Cinderella story, **7:45 PM**

Sports

BASEBALL
New York Mets vs.
Montreal Expos,
3:00 at Shea Stadium

CHARITY TENNIS
This year's Wimbledon
winners play to raise
money for disabled
children. 1 PM—7PM

3. OPENING AND CLOSING TIMES

✦ Could you	(please) tell me	when	*the store*	opens?
Can		what time		closes?

Role-play calling the places below to find out their opening and closing times. Take turns. Follow this model:

A: (calls the post office on the telephone)
B: Post office.
A: Hello. Could you tell me what time you open?
B: We open at 9:00.
A: And when do you close?
B: At 5:30.
A: Thank you.

Here is the information you need:

Post Office	9:00 a.m. —	5:30 p.m.
Citibank	9:00 —	5:00
Medical Clinic	9:30 —	8:00
Museum of Modern Art	11:00 —	6:00
Rexall Drugs	10:00 —	7:00
Macy's	10:00 —	9:30

▭ You are going to listen to information about when places open and close and when events start and end. Listen and fill in the blanks.

	Open / Start	Close / End
a) City Swimming Pool		
b) Casablanca		
Breakfast at Tiffany's		
Theater doors		
c) Rock 'n' roll concert		
Box office		

CONVERSATION 2
HOW DO I GET THERE?

Have you ever lost anything important? What did you do?
Have you ever gotten lost? What did you do?

OAK STREET

MAIN STREET

Police Station

Post Office

Pronunciation Focus

Words that carry stress in sentences are usually the words that carry important meaning in the sentence. Listen to the stressed words.

Do yóu know where the pólice station is?

No, I dón't. I'm nót from aróund here.

Now listen to the conversation again and mark the stressed words. Then practice the conversation.

Keith:	Excuse me, do you know where the police station is?
Woman:	No, I'm sorry. I don't. I'm not from around here.
Keith:	OK, thanks anyway.
Anna:	Hi, Keith! How's it going?
Keith:	Not too good. I lost my wallet, and it had all my ID and credit cards in it.
Anna:	Oh, no!
Keith:	So, how do I get to the police station from here?
Anna:	It's easy. Go up Main Street about three blocks. When you get to Oak Street, turn left. It's right next to the post office. You can't miss it.
Keith:	OK. Go up this street and turn left at Oak. It's beside the post office.
Anna:	That's it.
Keith:	Thanks, Anna.
Anna:	No problem.

1. DESCRIBING LOCATIONS

✦ Excuse me. | Do you know where the *hardware store* is?
| Could you tell me where the *hardware store* is?

✧ Sure. It's *on Elm Street,* | *across from the post office.*
| *between Eleventh and Twelfth Avenues.*

✦ Thank you.

✧ Sorry. I'm not sure.
✦ Thanks, anyway.

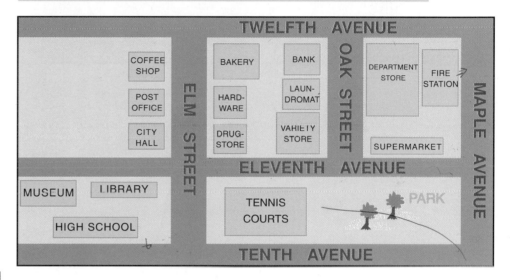

Practice

Ask your partner about the location of these places on the map. If you can't find the place, say that you don't know where it is.

Student A asks about:

1. city hall   3. camera store
2. laundromat   4. fire station

Student B asks about:

1. supermarket   3. post office
2. video store   4. park

2. GIVING DIRECTIONS

✦ Excuse me. | Which way is the | *camera store?*
| How do I get to the | *camera store* from here?

✧ It's down this street | on the *right.*
| just past the *Paris restaurant.*
Go up *two* blocks, and turn *right.*
Go up this street, and take the *second left.*

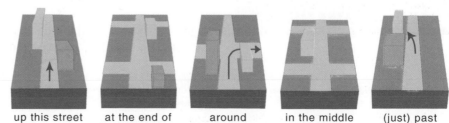

up this street   at the end of   around   in the middle   (just) past
on the left   the (next) block   the corner   of the block
                                        on the right

Look at the map below. Ask your partner how to get to the following places.
Student A starts out from location A (stadium).
Student B starts out from location B (bus station).

A wants to get to:
1. Citibank
2. Grace Hospital
3. Empire Cleaners
4. A-1 Car Rental

B wants to get to:
1. Bill's Variety Store
2. Spirit Women's Wear
3. St. Stephen's Church
4. Chinese Garden Restaurant

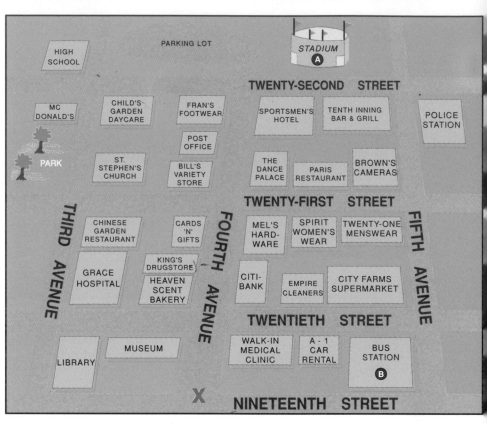

Ask your partner where you can do these things. Your partner will answer using the map above.

1. cash a traveler's check
2. fill a prescription
3. have some French food
4. buy a shirt and tie

5. get some film developed
6. buy a hammer and nails
7. buy some stamps
8. see a doctor without an appointment

Example:
Student A: Where can I buy a donut?
Student B: You can buy a donut at the bakery.

LISTEN TO THIS

▭ Start at Point X on the map above. Listen to the conversation and follow the directions. Then write down where each person is going.

Location 1...
Location 2...
Location 3...
Location 4...

PERSON TO PERSON

STUDENT A

(Student A looks at this page. Student B looks at the next page.)

Practice 1

Your partner will tell you about four errands he/she has for today. Decide which places your partner has to visit and give him/her directions using the map below.

Practice 2

You have four errands to do today. Tell your partner about all four. He/she will give you directions on the map below. As you arrive at each location, write the name. Your errands are:

cash a check
get a library card

get your coat cleaned
get some computer paper

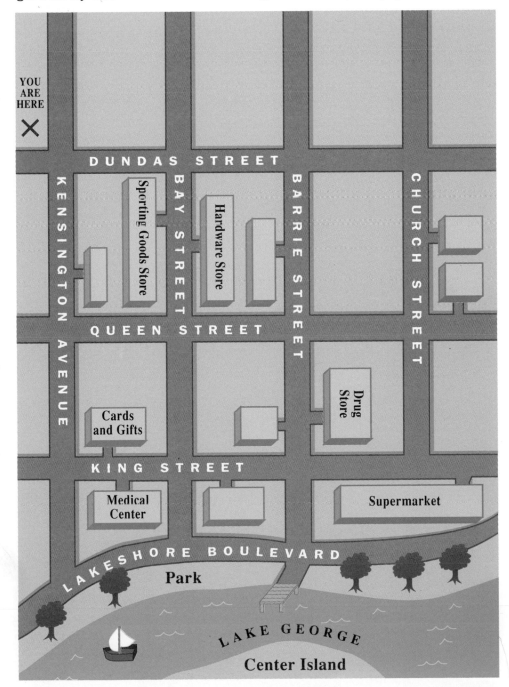

(Student B looks at this page. Student A looks at the previous page.)

Practice 1

You have four errands to do today. Tell your partner about all four. He/she will give you directions on the map below. As you arrive at each location, write the name. Your errands are:

buy a bicycle helmet   buy a birthday card
buy a first-aid kit   see the eye doctor

Practice 2

Your partner will tell you about four errands he/she has for today. Decide which places your partner has to visit and give him/her directions using the map below.

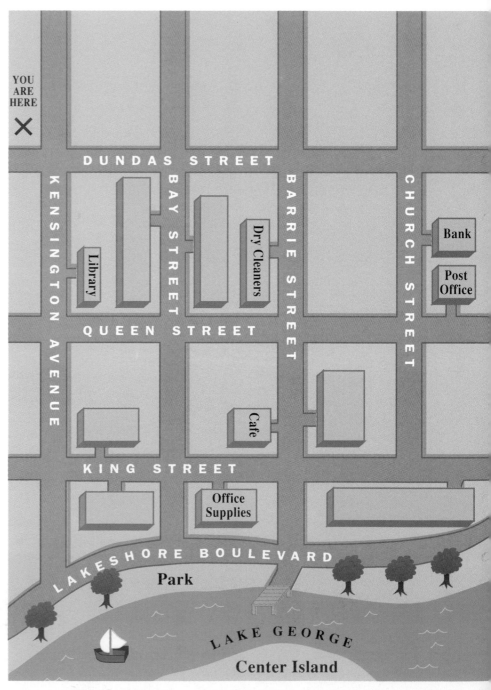

Do you like big cities?

What can you do in big cities?

Marta: So, what do you think? How do you like New York?

Paul: I'm having a great time. I love it. I'm glad we came.

Marta: Yeah. I really like the stores and the shopping.

Paul: I love the museums, too.

Marta: But the traffic is pretty bad.

Paul: Yeah. I hate all this traffic. It's really noisy.

Marta: Listen, it's almost dinnertime. There are lots of restaurants around here. What do you want to try? Italian? Greek? Japanese? Thai?

Paul: I can't stand making decisions. You choose!

Marta: OK. Let's go American. Where's the nearest McDonald's?

1. TALKING ABOUT LIKES AND DISLIKES

✦ How do you like	the *city?*		✦ Do you like	the *city?*
What do you think of	the *people?*			*New York?*

✧ I love	it.	✧ It's	OK.	✧ I can't stand it.
I really like			all right.	I hate it.
				I don't like it (at all).

Practice 1

Ask your partner if he/she likes the following things. Add three more of your own and ask about them.

If you don't know anything about the thing or activity, answer like this:

Student A asks about:

1. classical music
2. dogs
3. Mexican food
4. action movies
5. swimming
6. ....
7. ....
8. ....

Student B asks about:

1. playing golf
2. jazz
3. shopping for clothes
4. discos
5. watching TV
6. ....
7. ....
8. ....

Practice 2

Look at the list of things below. Mark your own likes and dislikes with a check (✔). Ask two other people about their likes and dislikes. Write in their names or initials.

?	love	like	OK	don't really like	hate/ can't stand
Big cities					
Pets					
Flying					
Watching TV					
Smokers					
Politicians					
Studying English					

Practice 3

Look at your chart. Decide which person you have the most in common with. Now, work with a classmate that you haven't spoken to yet. Report to each other what you found out.

LISTEN TO THIS

▭ Mary and Stan have decided to go out after work. They're talking about what to do. Write their opinions about the following topics.

	Mary	Stan
Chinese food	She didn't like	He sucks
hamburgers	I like it	be olc
musicals	Love musical	Hate
documentaries	sleep with	Love
bowling	she likes	good idea

What are these people planning to do?
Which activities do you like?

Pronunciation Focus

Listen and practice these words.

with [s]	with [sh]
sea	shore
sun	ocean
sand	fishing

Now practice the conversation.
Pay attention to the sounds [s] and [sh].

Tom: This one looks great! I love the seashore.

Ellen: So do I. The sun…the sand…the ocean!

Tom: And listen to this! What do you think of sailing, swimming, windsurfing, and fishing?

Ellen: Oh, Tom! They sound fantastic. I really like all those things.

Tom: Yeah…me, too.

Ellen: Well, except fishing. To be honest, I hate fishing, but I love all the others.

Tom: Hey! Look at this! We can stay in a big hotel or we can stay in a little cabin by the beach.

Ellen: You know, I really don't like those big hotels.

Tom: Neither do I. Let's stay in a cabin. It'll be much nicer right beside the ocean.

1. AGREEING AND DISAGREEING WITH LIKES AND DISLIKES

	AGREE	DISAGREE
◆ I love it. I like them. I hate it.	✧ Really? So do I. Me, too.	✧ You do? I don't. Really?
◆ I don't like them.	✧ (No.) Neither do I. Me neither.	✧ You don't? I do.
◆ I can't stand it.	✧ (No.) Neither can I. Me neither.	✧ You can't? | I like it. Really?

Practice 1

With your partner, decide whether the people below agree or disagree. Role-play their conversations. Then reverse roles.

Practice 2

Tell your partner two things you like, two things you don't like, two things you can't stand, and so on. Your partner will respond with a short answer.

2. STATING PREFERENCES

✦ I like *swimming*, but I don't like *diving*.
He likes *classical music*, but he can't stand *opera*.

Practice 1

Look at the lists below. Add three more choices in each category.

SPORTS	FOOD	MOVIES	MUSIC	ACTIVITIES	CHORES
baseball	Italian	musicals	rap	shopping	dusting
golf	French	comedies	jazz	eating out	vacuuming
soccer	Chinese	romance	classical	reading	laundry
volleyball	Indian	horror	heavy metal	listening to music	washing dishes
basketball	Japanese	action	rock 'n' roll	watching TV	cooking
_____	_____	_____	_____	_____	_____
_____	_____	_____	_____	_____	_____
_____	_____	_____	_____	_____	_____

Practice 2

Form small groups. Choose a category and talk about something that you like and don't like. Take turns until everyone has had a turn.

Example:
First Student: I like baseball, but I don't like volleyball.
Second Student: I love cooking, but I hate washing dishes.

LISTEN TO THIS

⬚ You are going to hear short conversations about likes and dislikes. Sometimes the speakers agree; sometimes they disagree. Check (✔) AGREE or DISAGREE as you listen to each one.

	Agree	Disagree
1.		
2.		
3.		
4.		

PERSON TO PERSON

STUDENT A

(Student A looks at this page. Student B looks at the next page.)

📼 You are going to hear a discussion between a man and a woman about movies and music. They refer to three famous filmmakers–Fellini, Bergman, and Kurosawa.

Practice 1

Listen to the conversation and check the man's likes and dislikes.

	Likes	Dislikes
a) Fellini		
b) Bergman		
c) Kurosawa		
d) Horror movies		
e) Heavy metal music		
f) Classical music		
g) Comedy movies		

Practice 2

Without turning the page, discuss the man's and woman's opinions with your partner.

Practice 3

Describe the following movie to your partner. Your partner will describe a movie to you. Decide which movie the man and woman should go to see.

The Phantom of the Opera–A beautiful French opera singer is kidnapped by an insane composer who lives beneath the Paris Opera House. This man with a terrible scar has killed before. Will she be his next victim?

(Student B looks at this page. Student A looks at the previous page.)

▭ You are going to hear a discussion between a man and a woman about movies and music. They refer to three famous filmmakers—Fellini, Bergman, and Kurosawa.

Practice 1

Listen to the conversation and check the woman's likes and dislikes.

	Likes	Dislikes
a) Fellini		
b) Bergman		
c) Kurosawa		
d) Horror movies		
e) Heavy metal music		
f) Classical music		
g) Comedy movies		

Practice 2

Without looking at the previous page, discuss the man's and woman's opinions with your partner.

Practice 3

Your partner will describe a movie to you. Then, describe the following movie to your partner. Decide which movie the man and woman should go to see.

Love and Death—This is Woody Allen's funniest film. He makes fun of love and death, politics, and serious foreign films. There is a lot of beautiful classical music by Prokofiev.

WOODY ALLEN   DIANE KEATON

The Comedy Sensation of the Year!

"LOVE and DEATH"

At what age do young people begin dating in your country?

What are some typical "dating rules"?

Do young people prefer to date in groups or by themselves?

Debbie: Hi, Kenji.

Kenji: Hi, Debbie. Have a seat. How's it going?

Debbie: I'm OK. How are you doing?

Kenji: Pretty good. Listen . . . have you heard about the new Thai restaurant over on University Avenue?

Debbie: Do you mean The Bangkok?

Kenji: That's the one. A bunch of us are going there for dinner tomorrow night. How about coming with us?

Debbie: Sure, I'd love to.

Kenji: Great. I'll call and make reservations.

Debbie: Any time after 6:00 is good for me. Oh! I'm late! I have a class.

Kenji: All right. I'll call you tonight and tell you the time.

Debbie: Great. Talk to you then.

1. ACCEPTING INVITATIONS

✦ Do you feel like	*going out for dinner*	*Saturday?*
What about		*tonight?*
How about		

✧ Sure.	I'd love to.
OK.	That's a great idea.
	Why not?
	That's a good idea.

Practice

Invite your partner to do the following things. Your partner agrees. Find out if he/she feels like:

1. going out for dinner next Friday
2. seeing a movie Sunday afternoon
3. going for coffee
4. playing tennis
5. going camping

Add some ideas of your own.

2. DECLINING INVITATIONS

| ✦ Do | you | want to | *have lunch tomorrow?* |
| Would | | like to | |

| ✧ Oh, | I'm sorry. I can't. | I have to | *meet a friend.* |
| | I'm afraid | I've got to | |

✦ That's too bad. Maybe next time.

Practice

Invite your partner to do the following things. He/she is busy and makes an excuse. Then reverse roles. Add ideas of your own to each list.

Invitations

1. go to a party tonight
2. see a movie Friday night
3. go golfing on Sunday
4. go shopping on Saturday
5. ....
6. ....

Excuses

1. work late
2. meet a friend
3. visit my parents
4. go to a meeting
5. ....
6. ....

3. GETTING MORE INFORMATION

✦ Would you like to | *go to a party this Saturday?*
  Do you want to |

✧ Sounds good. | *What kind of party?*
               | *Where is it?*
               | *Who's going?*

✦ It's *a birthday party/potluck dinner.*
  It's *at my place/Dave's.*
  Some people from work/school.

Practice

Invite your partner to the following events. Your partner will ask for extra information. Take turns. Fill in the blanks with your own ideas/information.

Event	Information requested	Information
1. potluck dinner	What can I bring?	It's up to you.
2. baseball game	Who's playing?	Blue Jays and Yankees
3. dinner	What time?	8 o'clock
4. go for a drive	Where?	in the country
5. see a movie	Which movie?	....
6. go swimming	....	....
7.	....	....
8.	....	....

LISTEN TO THIS

▭ You are going to hear two conversations. Listen and finish each sentence.

1. Ted and Diane

a) Diane wants to ....
b) Ted wants to...
c) Club Blue Note serves mostly...........................and ....
d) The prices at the club are ....

2. Ben and Oscar

a) Ben invites Oscar to a..
b) Oscar can't go because he has to go ....
c) Oscar can go after..
d) Oscar will bring..
e) They will .... for dinner.

CONVERSATION 2
WHY DON'T WE MEET THERE?

Is it all right for a woman to ask a man for a date?
Do women ask men for dates very often?
Are there any special days when women ask men out?

Karen: Hello. Could I speak to Justin, please?

Justin: Speaking.

Karen: Oh, hi Justin. This is Karen Hepburn. We met at Chris and Jim's party.

Justin: Of course. How're you?

Karen: Great. Uh, Justin, would you like to see Otis Isley on Thursday night? He's at the Kangaroo Club.

Justin: I'm sorry, Karen, but I can't. I have to work late this Thursday.

Karen: Oh… that's too bad.

Justin: Yeah. I really like Isley.

Karen: Actually, are you doing anything on Friday or Saturday? He's playing those two nights as well.

Justin: Well, I can't make it on Friday either, but I'm free on Saturday night. What time does it start?

Karen: At eight sharp. How about meeting in front of the club at about a quarter after seven?

Justin: That sounds perfect. And let's go out for coffee after the show.

Karen: Sure!

Justin: OK, see you at 7:15, Saturday.

Pronunciation Focus

Often one word in a sentence is more important than others and is stressed more heavily than the other words in the sentence. Listen.

Could I speak to Justin please?

I have to work late this Thursday.

Listen to the conversation again and mark the stressed words. Then practice the conversation.

1. SUGGESTING ANOTHER DAY

✦ I'm really sorry. I can't make it.	
✧ OK. Maybe we can do it some other time then.	✧ Well, how about *Friday*, then?
✦ Yes, I'd really like to.	✦ Great! That sounds good.

Practice 1

Invite your partner to do something. He/she is busy and can't accept. Respond to the refusal.

Practice 2

Invite your partner to do something. He/she is busy and can't accept. Suggest another time.

2. SETTING THE TIME AND PLACE

✦ Where do you want to meet?

✧ How about meeting | *in front of the club?*
Why don't we meet | *at the restaurant?*
Let's meet *at the restaurant.*

✦ Great. What time?

✧ How about meeting | at | *7:15?*
Why don't we meet | |
Is *7:15* OK?
Let's meet at *7:15.*

✦ Fine.
OK. See you | *at 7:15.*
 | *then.*

Practice

Invite your partner to do something. He/she accepts. Set the time and place.

3. CHANGING PLANS

✦ Could we meet | at the subway instead?
_____ | at 7:00?
_____ | a little later?
_____ | earlier?

✧ Sure. That's no problem.

Practice

Invite your partner to do something and arrange a time and place to meet. Your partner will suggest a different time or place. Then reverse roles.

4. ADDING TO PLANS

✦ We could | go for coffee after the show.
Let's ___ | go out dancing after dinner.

✧ Do you want to | have dinner before the movie?
Why don't we _ | go swimming after we play tennis?

Practice

Student A invites **Student B** to do two of the following. **Student B** suggests adding to the plan. Then reverse roles. Add some ideas of your own.

A's invitations:

1. go sailing
2. go for a drive in the country
3. meet downtown for lunch
4. come over and watch videos

B's suggestions:

1. have lunch first
2. stop somewhere for brunch
3. do some shopping afterward
4. order a pizza for dinner

LISTEN TO THIS

🔊 Barry is arranging an evening out with his friend, Andrew. Listen and answer the questions.

1. What does Barry want to do? ....
2. What time does Barry suggest? ....
3. What else does Andrew want to do? ....
4. What time are they going to meet? ....
5. Where are they going to meet? ....

PERSON TO PERSON

STUDENT A

(Student A looks at this page. Student B looks at the next page.)

▭ Carmen and Yoshiko want to get together sometime this week, but they're having difficulty finding a time when both of them are free.

Practice 1

Listen and fill in Carmen's appointment book.

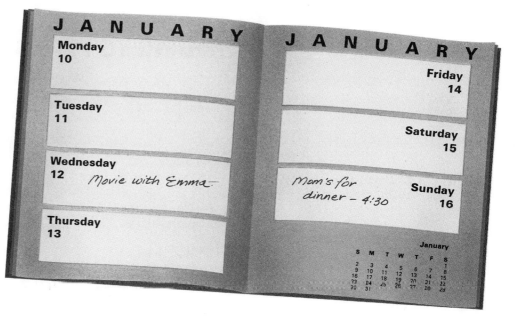

Practice 2

Review the times that Carmen and Yoshiko are both busy. Then continue their conversation. Find out when they are both free. Decide what type of restaurant they'll go to, and arrange a place and a time to meet.

(Student B looks at this page. Student A looks at the previous page.)

Carmen and Yoshiko want to get together sometime this week, but they're having difficulty finding a time when both of them are free.

Practice 1

Listen and fill in Yoshiko's appointment book.

J A N U A R Y

Monday 10

Tuesday 11

Wednesday 12

Thursday 13

J A N U A R Y

Friday 14

Saturday 15

Cleaning and packing — all day! **Sunday 16**

January

S	M	T	W	T	F	S
2	3	4	5	6	7	1 8
9	10	11	12	13	14	15
16	17	18	19	20	21	22
23	24	25	26	27	28	29
30	31					

Practice 2

Review the times that Carmen and Yoshiko are both busy. Then continue their conversation. Find out when they are both free. Decide what type of restaurant they'll go to, and arrange a place and a time to meet.

Do you like shopping?
Do you prefer department stores or specialty shops?
Do you like to pay cash or use a charge card? Why?

Clerk:	Hi. Can I help you with something?
Paulina:	Yes, please. We're looking for the men's department.
Clerk:	It's right over there, by the escalator.
Diego:	Here we are... and here are the sport shirts.
Paulina:	Look at this one. The color is perfect for you!
Diego:	I like it, too. How much is it?
Paulina:	It's on sale for $19.98.
Diego:	That's a good price. But I think they only have it in large.
Paulina:	Excuse me! Could you help me?
Clerk:	Sure. What can I do for you?
Paulina:	Does this shirt come in medium?
Clerk:	Yes, it does. Here's a medium.
Diego:	Great. We'll take it.
Clerk:	Will that be cash or charge?

1. GETTING AND GIVING HELP

✦ Excuse me. | Could | you help me?
| Can |

✧ Certainly. | What can I help you with?
Sure. | What can I do for you?

✦ Can I help you with something?
Is there something I can help you with?

✧ No, thanks. I'm just looking.
Yes, please. I'm looking for the *men's sweaters*.

Practice 1

You are shopping in a department store. Your partner is a sales clerk. Ask him/her for help.

Practice 2

You are a clerk in a department store. Your partner is a customer. Ask if he/she needs help.

2. GETTING INFORMATION

✦ Do you | have | this | in *size 10?*   ✧ Yes, we do.
| carry | these | in *green?*   No, I'm sorry. We don't.

✦ Does this | come in | *medium?*   ✧ Yes, | *it does.*
Do these | | *beige?* | *they do.*
| | *size 8?*
| | a | *larger* | size?   ✧ No, I'm sorry. | *It doesn't.*
| | | *smaller* | | *They don't.*

Practice

Your partner is a salesperson. Get his/her attention and ask for information about two of the items below. Then reverse roles.

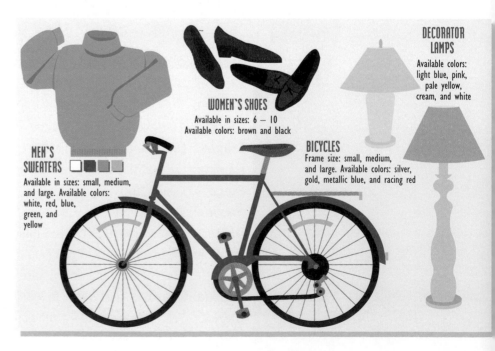

DECORATOR LAMPS
Available colors: light blue, pink, pale yellow, cream, and white

WOMEN'S SHOES
Available in sizes: 6 – 10
Available colors: brown and black

BICYCLES
Frame size: small, medium, and large. Available colors: silver, gold, metallic blue, and racing red

MEN'S SWEATERS
Available in sizes: small, medium, and large. Available colors: white, red, blue, green, and yellow

3. ASKING PRICES

◆ How much	is *this (radio)/it?*		✧ (It's)	*$59.98.*
	are *these (speakers)/they?*		(They're)	*$299.*
Could	you tell me the price of	*this radio?*	(It's)	*$129.*
Can		*these speakers?*	(They're)	*$600.*

Practice 1

Ask your partner the price of four of the following items. Then reverse roles.

Student A	**Student B**
1. shoes	1. $59.95
2. CD player	2. $299
3. pen	3. $1.59
4. postcards	4. 10 for $1
5. silk jacket	5. $235
6. T-shirts	6. 3 for $19
7. cassette tape	7. $7.99
8. silver picture frame	8. $89.98

Practice 2

Ask classmates for the prices of four items that you often buy in your city. Use the list below or think of your own.

1. a cup of coffee
2. bus fare from home to school
3. a CD
4. a Coke

5. a movie ticket
6. an ice cream cone
7. a video rental
8. a pack of gum

LISTEN TO THIS

A man and his wife are in a department store buying Christmas gifts for their three children. Listen and write down the information they get from the sales clerk. Put a check (✔) if they buy the item.

	Ski Jacket	**Leather gloves**	**Golf bags**
Size needed	10	medium	small
Size available	4, 6, 8, 10	small, med, lar	large
Color wanted	pink	green	
Color available	red, pink, grey	blank, brown	black, white, blodgrong
Price	160	50	150
Bought Item	the going thing alsrow	toke brown	

Why do you return things to a store?

What is an exchange?

What is a refund?

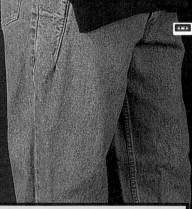

Allen: Excuse me. Could you help me? I'd like to exchange this sweater.

Clerk: What's the problem with it?

Allen: It was a birthday gift, but I don't really like it. I think I want something plainer.

Clerk: I see . . . Well, why don't you look around?

Marta: I like these two, Allen. Try them on.

Allen: OK. So, which one do you like?

Marta: I like the red one much better than the black one.

Allen: Really? How come? I kind of like the black one.

Marta: The red one is longer and a little looser so it will be more comfortable.

Allen: True . . . and it feels softer.

Clerk: And that color looks better on you. Actually, it's a better quality and it's the same price as the sweater you're exchanging.

Allen: You've talked me into it! I'll take this one instead.

Clerk: No problem. I'll switch them for you.

Pronunciation Focus

In American and Canadian English, *r* is pronounced after a vowel. Listen and practice these words.

sweater	more	birthday
plainer	looser	softer
longer	better	color

1. COMPARING THINGS (1)

✦ Which | *hat* | do you like better?
         | *boots* |

✧ I like | *the green hat* | better than | *the yellow* one.
         | *this hat* | | *that* one.

✧ I like | *the red boots* | better than | *the white* ones.
         | *these boots* | | *those.*

Ask your partner which one(s) he/she prefers.

2. COMPARING THINGS (2)

✦ Why do you like *the green hat* better?
✧ (I like it) because it's *fancier* than the *yellow* one.

✦ Why do you like the *red boots* better?
✧ (I like them) because they're *more stylish* than the *white* ones.

Look at the pictures above. Ask your partner which item(s) he/she prefers, and then ask why. Then reverse roles. Ask and answer like this:

Student A: Which .... do you like better?
Student B: I like the .... better than the .... one(s).
Student A: Why? / How come?
Student B: Because ....

Here are some possible reasons:

fancier/plainer, bigger/smaller, longer/shorter, looser/tighter,
more expensive/less expensive, more colorful, more comfortable, a nicer color,
brighter, softer, better quality

3. RETURNING THINGS

◆ I'd like | a refund, | please.
| to get a refund,
| to return this *(sweater)*,
| to exchange this *(blouse)*,

◇ What's | the reason?
| the problem with it?

◆ It's | *too big/small.*
| *the wrong color.*
It doesn't fit.
It was a gift. I already have one.
I don't really like it.

◇ Of course. We can | exchange it.
| give you a refund.
I'm sorry. There are no refunds or exchanges.

Practice

Your partner is a sales clerk. Choose two of the items below and ask for a refund or an exchange. Then reverse roles.

LISTEN TO THIS

📟 Three customers have items to return to a department store. Listen and write down the things they want to return, the reason, and the result.

	Item	Reason	Result
Customer 1	coat	to small	return
Customer 2	tape	to knowusy	no exchange
Customer 3	sweater	don't like color	swip switch

PERSON TO PERSON

STUDENT A

(Student A looks at this page. Student B looks at the next page.)

Kerry is going to Europe this summer for two weeks and needs to buy some new clothes. Listen as she and her friend, Joan, compare each item.

Practice 1

Write down Joan's comments.

Black pants ....
Pink pants ....
Purple sweater ....
White sweater ....
Suede jacket ....
Cotton jacket ....

Discuss Joan and Kerry's comments with your partner. Which items do you think Kerry will buy?

Practice 2

Ask your partner questions to get information about the suitcase below. Your partner will ask you about the garment bag.

Suitcase
Materials: ....
Sizes: ....
....
Prices: ....
....
Colors: ....
....

Garment bag
Materials: Nylon and leather
Sizes: Regular (39"Hx24"Wx3"D)
          Long (47"Hx24.5"Wx3.5"D)
Prices: Regular $160
          Long $170
Colors: Burgundy, Navy, Green,
          Black

Practice 3

Kerry will be traveling by plane, train, and car. She only wants to carry one piece of luggage. Look at the descriptions above and decide with your partner which piece she should buy.

(Student B looks at this page. Student A looks at the previous page.)

▭ Kerry is going to Europe this summer for two weeks and needs to buy some new clothes. Listen as she and her friend, Joan, compare each item.

Practice 1

Write down Kerry's comments.

Black pants ....
Pink pants ....
Purple sweater ....
White sweater ....
Suede jacket ....
Cotton jacket ....

Discuss Joan and Kerry's comments with your partner. Which items do you think Kerry will buy?

Practice 2

Ask your partner questions to get information about the garment bag below. Your partner will ask you about the suitcase.

Suitcase
Materials: Nylon and leather
Sizes: Regular (15"Hx21.5"Lx9"D)
            Large (19.5"Hx25.5"Lx9"D)
Prices: Regular $84
            Large $105
Colors: Burgundy, Navy, Green,
            Black

Garment bag
Materials:..
Sizes: ....
....
Prices:..
....
Colors: ....
....

Practice 3

Kerry will be traveling by plane, train, and car. She only wants to carry one piece of luggage. Look at the descriptions above and decide with your partner which piece she should buy.

How often do you eat out at restaurants?
What is your favorite kind of restaurant?

Ted: Everything looks good. What are you going to have, Julie?

Julie: I think I'll have the spaghetti and a salad. How about you? What are you having?

Ted: Spaghetti sounds good, but I feel like a steak. I guess we're ready to order. Excuse me!

Waitress: Good evening. Have you decided yet?

Julie: Yes. I'll have the spaghetti and a salad.

Waitress: And what kind of dressing would you like on your salad?

Julie: I'd like oil and vinegar.

Waitress: OK. And what would you like, sir?

Ted: I'd like a steak, medium-rare, please.

Waitress: Would you like soup or salad with that?

Ted: What kind of soup do you have tonight?

Waitress: Cream of mushroom and clam chowder.

Ted: Clam chowder, please. And I'll have a baked potato and carrots.

Waitress: I'll be right back with your soup and salad.

Julie: Thank you.

1. DISCUSSING THE MENU

✦ What are you │ going to have, │ *Julie?*
                │ having,

✧ (I think) I'll have *the spaghetti* and *a salad*.

You're at a restaurant having breakfast with a friend. Ask what he/she wants to eat and drink. He/she answers using the cues below.

1. scrambled eggs, home fries, and wheat toast/tea
2. a cheese omelette and sausages/a large glass of milk
3. some cereal/a small glass of orange juice/some cocoa
4. fried eggs and bacon/a large glass of apple juice
5. the blueberry pancakes/coffee

Try it again. This time, choose from the menu below.

GOOD MORNING MENU

Breakfast served from 7:00 to 11:30 A.M.

EGGS & OMELETTES

Eggs (2) **$3.95**
Fried, Scrambled, Poached or Boiled

Omelettes **$4.95**
*Fluffy 3 egg omelette-
Ham, Cheese or Western*

All egg orders are served with bacon or toast.

OTHER SPECIALTIES

Pancakes **$5.25**
Waffles **$5.25**
French Toast **$4.75**

FROM OUR BAKE SHOP

Fresh Muffins **$1.50**
Bran, Blueberry, or Oatmeal

Croissant **$2.50**
Served with jam

Toast **$1.25**
Served with jam

BEVERAGES

Juice ....
*small... .75 large... **$1.25***
*Orange, Apple, Tomato or
Grapefruit*

Milk ....
*small... .85 large... **$1.50***

Pot of Tea.................... **$1.25**
Coffee........................ **$1.00**
Cocoa......................... **$1.75**

2. ORDERING

✦ What │ would you │ like, *ma'am?*
        │ will   │ have, *sir?*
  Are you ready to order, │ *miss?*
  Have you decided yet,   │

✧ I'd like │ *a steak, medium-rare*, please.
  I'll have │
  Could we have a few more minutes, please?

Look at the menu again. Choose something and the waiter/waitress will take your order.

3. SPECIFYING WANTS

✦ What kind of *dressing* would you like?

✧ I'll | have | *creamy garlic* (please).
  | take
  I'd like |

✦ Would you like *soup* or *salad*?

✧ I'd like *soup*, please.

•Menu•

TODAY'S LUNCH SPECIALS
Chicken Fingers
Juicy strips of tender white meat deep-fried in crispy batter
Crab and Asparagus Quiche
Made with real crab meat and tender, young asparagus tips
Hot Roast Beef Sandwich
Thick slices of beef, cut fresh from the roast
Breaded Filet of Sole
Fresh sole, rolled lightly in bread crumbs, and baked to flaky perfection

All specials come with your choice of:
-Cream of Mushroom Soup or Green Salad
(French or Oil & Vinegar Dressing)
-Potatoes: Baked, Mashed or French Fries
-Vegetables: Buttered or Glazed Carrots
-Dessert: Vanilla Ice Cream or Fresh Fruit

Practice 1

Student A:
You are the waiter/waitress. Ask the customer about the following items.

1. soup or salad
2. dressing for your salad
3. potatoes
4. vegetables
5. dessert

Student B:
You are the customer. Choose from today's lunch specials.

Practice 2

Role-play a restaurant scene. Take turns being the waiter/waitress and customer. Begin like this:

A: Excuse me!

B: Yes, sir/ma'am. What would you like?

LISTEN TO THIS

A family is having dinner at their local fast-food restaurant. Listen and write down what each person orders.

Davey	
Father	
Mother	

Do you take a long time to decide what to order in a restaurant?

Do you like to try new foods?

What new foods do you want to try?

Waiter: OK, so that's one cheeseburger and one order of chicken wings, extra spicy. Would you like something to drink with that?

Carol: Do you have any diet Coke?

Waiter: I'm sorry, we don't. We have diet Pepsi.

Carol: I'll have that, then.

Linda: Make it two.

Waiter: Would you like to have your Pepsi now?

Linda: Yes, please.

Carol: No, thank you. I'll wait for my cheeseburger.

Waiter: And would you care for any dessert?

Linda: No thanks. I'm sure I'll be full.

Carol: They have fantastic chocolate cheesecake here...

Linda: They do? Well, maybe we could split some.

Waiter: Would you like me to bring two forks?

Carol: Yes, please. Good idea.

Pronunciation Focus

We pronounce *would you* like *wouldya*. Listen to these questions, then practice them.

Would you like something to drink?
Would you like to have your Pepsi now?
Would you care for any dessert?

Now practice the conversation. Pay attention to *would you*.

1. ASKING ABOUT WANTS

✦ Would you	care for	anything	to drink?
	like	something	
Can I get you			

✧ Do you have any *iced tea?*

✦ I'm	afraid	we don't.	✦ Yes, certainly.
	sorry,	we're all out.	
		we've run out.	

| ✧ (I'll have) a *Coke*, then. | ✧ I'd like some, | please. |
| | I'll have that, | |

Practice

Student A (customer)
Ask for the following drinks.
If they are not available,
choose something else.

1. iced tea/ice coffee
2. lemonade
3. 7 Up/Coke
4. milk/hot chocolate
5. ginger ale/Pepsi
6. espresso/cafe au lait →Strong Coffe.

Student B (waiter/waitress)
To answer, look at this list.

NOT AVAILABLE TODAY
Iced Tea
Ginger Ale
Cocoa
7-Up
Iced Coffee

2. OFFERING SERVICE

✦ Shall I bring	your *coffee* (now)?
Would you like me to get	
Would you like (to have)	
Would you like some more *coffee?*	

✧ Yes, please.
No, thank you.

Practice

Ask if the customer would like the following:

1. some coffee/tea
2. a glass of water
3. an extra plate
4. two forks with the dessert
5. some ketchup
6. extra cream for the coffee

3. ASKING ABOUT OTHER WANTS

✦ Would you | like | anything else?
           | care for | some *dessert?*

✧ No, thank you.
  Not right now, thank you.
  Yes, could you bring me | some more *rolls?*
                          | some *chocolate cheesecake?*

  Just the | bill, | please.
           | check, |

Practice

Student A: Ask the customer **(B)** if he/she wants anything else.

Student B: You can choose a dessert from the list below or decline if you don't want one.

Desserts

Pies: apple, cherry, peach, pecan
Cakes: chocolate, carrot, cheesecake
Ice Cream: chocolate, vanilla, rum raisin, coffee
Mousse: double chocolate, strawberry, lemon

LISTEN TO THIS

▭ Listen to the conversations. Write down the thing(s) that the waiter/waitress is going to bring.

Conversation 1 ....

Conversation 2 ....

Conversation 3 ....

(Student A looks at this page. Student B looks at the next page.)

You are going to hear a couple ordering dinner. As you listen, look at the menu.

Practice 1

Write (W) for woman next to the choices she makes. The man's choices are marked for you.

Well dan medium well medium wrare

MENU

ENTREES

m **NEW YORK SIRLOIN STEAK**
broiled to sizzling perfection

HALIBUT CREOLE
fresh halibut cooked in a zesty *(smashed condiments)* sauce of tomatoes, onions, and green peppers

SALMON TERIYAKI
fresh Atlantic salmon with a taste of the Orient

LOBSTER TAILS
served with melted butter, lemon wedges and a bib

BARBECUED CHICKEN
tender breast of chicken with our spicy barbecue sauce from a secret family recipe

All of the above entrees are served with your choice of

Potato (*m* mashed, ___ boiled or ___ baked)
Vegetable (___ broccoli, *m* asparagus ___ peas & carrots)
and
Soup of the day (ask your server about today's soup)
or
Salad (___ French, ___ blue cheese or ___ oil & vinegar dressing)

Beverage (___ coffee, *m* iced coffee, ___ tea or ___ iced tea)
Dessert (___ ice cream, ___ French pastry or ___ fresh fruit)

What extra request does the woman have? ....

Check your answers with your partner.

Practice 2

Join another pair of students. Using the menu above, one of you will take the part of the waiter/waitress. The rest of you will look at the menu and discuss what you're going to have. Then call the waiter/waitress and place your order. If you have time, reverse roles.

Guest Check

Thank you – Call Again

TABLE	NO. PERSONS	WAITER / WAITRESS			

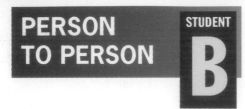

PERSON TO PERSON

STUDENT B

(Student B looks at this page. Student A looks at the previous page.)

You are going to hear a couple ordering dinner. As you listen, look at the menu.

Practice 1

Write (M) for man next to the choices he makes. The woman's choices are marked for you.

MENU
ENTREES

—— **NEW YORK SIRLOIN STEAK**
broiled to sizzling perfection

—— **HALIBUT CREOLE**
fresh halibut cooked in a zesty sauce of tomatoes, onions and green peppers

W **SALMON TERIYAKI**
fresh Atlantic salmon with a taste of the Orient

—— **LOBSTER TAILS**
served with melted butter, lemon wedges and a bib

—— **BARBECUED CHICKEN**
tender breast of chicken with our spicy barbecue sauce from a secret family recipe

All of the above entrees are served with your choice of

Potato (____ mashed, ____ boiled or *W* baked)
Vegetable (*W* broccoli, ____ asparagus ____ peas & carrots)
and
Soup of the day (ask your server about today's soup)
or
Salad (____ French, ____ blue cheese or *W* oil & vinegar dressing)

Beverage (____ coffee, *W* iced coffee, ____ tea or ____ iced tea)
Dessert (____ ice cream, ____ French pastry or ____ fresh fruit)

What extra request does the man have? ....

Check your answers with your partner.

Practice 2

Join another pair of students. Using the menu above, one of you will take the part of the waiter/waitress. The rest of you will look at the menu and discuss what you're going to have. Then call the waiter/waitress and place your order. If you have time, reverse roles.

Guest Check

Thank you – Call Again

TABLE	NO. PERSONS	WAITER / WAITRESS		

Do friends sometimes borrow things from you? What things?
Are there some things you don't like to lend? What are they?

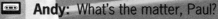

Andy: What's the matter, Paul?

Paul: Can you believe this? I locked my keys in the car, and I have to go to the airport to pick up my aunt.

Andy: So, what are you going to do?

Paul: I don't know... Hey, do you think I could borrow your car for a few hours?

Andy: I'm sorry, but I really need it this afternoon.

Paul: Well, could you drive me home? I have spare keys there.

Andy: Sure. That's no problem.

Paul: Oh, and Andy? Do you have a quarter for the phone? My wallet's in the car.

Andy: Here you go. Anything else?

Paul: No, that's it. Thanks. I really appreciate it.

1. MAKING SMALL REQUESTS

✦ Do you have an extra	pencil?
Could I borrow a	piece of paper?
	tissue?
	quarter?

| ✧ Sure. Here you | are. | ✧ I'm sorry. I don't have | one. |
| | go. | | any. |

Practice 1

Ask for four of the following items. Your partner can agree or refuse. Make sure to give reasons for refusals. Then reverse roles.

1. pen
2. pencil
3. dime
4. dictionary

5. piece of paper
6. ruler
7. quarter
8. eraser

Practice 2

Think of four small things you want to borrow. Move around the class and ask your classmates. When you have all four things, return to your seat.

2. MAKING LARGER REQUESTS

| ✦ Do you think I could borrow | $25 until Tuesday? |
| Would you mind lending me | your watch for a few hours? |

✧ Sure.	✧ I'm sorry.	I don't have $25.
OK.		I need it right now.
	Can I let you know later?

Practice 1

Make four requests. Your partner can agree or refuse. Be sure to give reasons for refusals. Then reverse roles.

1. car for the afternoon
2. $100 until next Friday
3. computer for the weekend
4. sleeping bag for a week

5. videotape machine tonight
6. new motorcycle for an hour
7. lawnmower on Sunday
8. CD player for a party
   on Saturday night

Practice 2

Now practice the exercise again. This time, think of your own requests.

3. ASKING FOR FAVORS

✦ Would you (please) | get the | *door?*	
Could you | | *lights?*	
| | *hold my coat for a minute?*	
✧ Sure. (No problem.)	✧ I'm sorry. I can't right now.
Of course.	
I'd be glad to.	

Practice 1

Ask your partner to do three of these favors for you. Your partner agrees to do each favor. Use the following, and then reverse roles.

1. open the window
2. turn up the volume
3. carry my books

4. hold my books for a second
5. explain the homework after class
6. check my homework

Practice 2

Think of some interesting or unusual favors. Move around the room and ask your classmates. They can agree or refuse.

LISTEN TO THIS

▭ Listen to the conversations. Put the number of the conversation on the correct line.

Have you ever had problems at a hotel?

What happened?

What did you do?

Pronunciation Focus

Notice how we pronounce *can* and *can't*.

can [kən]	can't [kænt]
What can I do for you?	I can't stand it.

Now practice the conversation. Pay attention to *can* and *can't*.

Guest: Excuse me.

Clerk: Yes? What can I do for you?

Guest: I just checked in, and there's a problem with my room.

Clerk: And what is the problem?

Guest: I asked for a non-smoking room, and I don't have one. My room smells like cigarette smoke. I can't stand it. Could you change my room, please.

Clerk: Let me see. . . I'm sorry, but we don't have any more non-smoking rooms. We won't charge you for your room tonight.

Guest: Thank you.

Clerk: I'm very sorry about this.

Guest: That's OK. Thanks for your help.

1. COMPLAINING POLITELY

✦ Excuse me. Sorry to bother you, but Could you help me?	I have a problem with	*my room.* *my seat.*

✧ What's the problem?
What seems to be the problem?

✦ *I asked for a non-smoking room.*
I requested the non-smoking section.

Practice 1

Student A is a hotel guest and **Student B** is the front desk clerk. **Student A** makes the following complaints.

1. asked for an ocean view/can only see the parking lot
2. asked for single beds/got a double bed
3. asked for a double room/got a single room

Practice 2

Student B is a passenger on a long flight and **Student A** is a flight attendant. **Student B** makes the following complaints.

1. asked for a seat in the non-smoking section/got smoking
2. asked for an aisle seat/got a window seat
3. asked to sit near the front of the plane/got the tail

2. REQUESTING ACTION OR A CHANGE

✦ Could you change *my room*, please?	
✧ I can change *your room* tomorrow. I'd be glad to.	✧ I'm sorry, I can't.

Practice

Student A: You are staying in a nice hotel, but there are a few things wrong. Identify the problem and request action.

Student B: Agree to the request and say when the action can be taken.

Take turns role-playing.

Problem	**Solution**
1. not enough towels	1. send more towels
2. the room is too hot	2. fix the air conditioner
3. noisy people next door	3. ask them to be quiet
4. the toilet won't flush	4. send someone to fix it

3. ACCEPTING AN APOLOGY

✦ I'm (very) sorry about this.

✧ That's | OK. | Thanks for your help.
It's | | It wasn't your fault.
| | Don't worry about it.

Practice

Now put it all together. With your partner, choose one of the following problems and prepare a conversation. One of you will complain, request action, and accept an apology. Then choose another problem and reverse roles.

1. at a dry-cleaners: your jacket still isn't clean
2. at a camera store: they reprinted the wrong photos
3. at a video store: the movie was blank in the middle
4. at a restaurant: the bill was added incorrectly

LISTEN TO THIS

You are going to hear conversations with two people who have complaints to make. Listen and answer the following questions.

Conversation 1

1. What is the woman's complaint?..
2. What action does she request?...
3. Where is the woman?...

Conversation 2

1. What is the woman's complaint?..
2. What action does she request?...
3. How much is her new bill?..

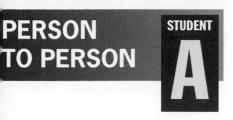
(Student A looks at this page. Student B looks at the next page.)

Practice 1

You and your partner are on vacation in Hawaii for one week. Unfortunately, the airline lost your partner's luggage. Your partner will ask you for four favors. Agree to do some, but refuse to do others. Be sure to give reasons when you refuse.

Your information:

- you speak English very well
- your clothes won't fit your partner
- you didn't bring any suntan lotion
- you love shopping

Decide with your partner what actions you can take to solve any other problems you might have.

Practice 2

You're having a bad day today. You overslept, left home in a hurry, and forgot your book bag and wallet. You made plans to meet a friend right after school for a game of tennis and then dinner. Ask your partner to do these favors. Put a (✔) beside the ones he/she can help you with.

You want your partner to:

- lend you some paper and a pen (your supplies are all at home)
- drive you home at lunch (you can get the things you forgot)
- lend you his tennis racquet (you don't have your tennis equipment)
- lend you $25 to pay for dinner (you can pay it back tomorrow)

Decide with your partner what actions you can take to solve any other problems you might have.

PERSON TO PERSON

STUDENT B

(Student B looks at this page. Student A looks at the previous page.)

Practice 1

You and your partner are visiting Hawaii for a week. Your problem is that the airline lost your luggage. Everything you need is in your suitcases. Ask your partner to do these favors. Put a (✔) beside the ones he/she can help you with.

You want your partner to:

- call the airline for you (you're too shy)
- lend you some clothes (you're hot and uncomfortable)
- lend you some suntan lotion (yours is in the lost luggage)
- go shopping with you to buy clothes (you need something to wear)

Decide with your partner what actions you can take to solve any other problems you might have.

Practice 2

Your partner overslept today, arrived late, and forgot to bring his/her book bag and wallet. Your partner is going to meet another friend right after class for a game of tennis and then dinner. Your partner will ask you for four favors. Agree to do some, but refuse to do others. Be sure to give reasons when you refuse.

Your information:

- you have extra paper and pens
- you have only $20 but your bank is right around the corner
- you didn't bring your car today
- your tennis equipment is in your locker

Decide with your partner what actions you can take to solve any other problems you might have.

Do people in your country move around a lot?
Is it a good idea for families to move from city to city?
How about from country to country?

Brad: So, Paula, where are you from?

Paula: I'm from Canada, originally.

Brad: From Canada? Where were you born?

Paula: Montreal.

Brad: When did you come to Los Angeles?

Paula: We moved here when I was fourteen.

Brad: Did you go to school here?

Paula: Well, I went to high school here, but I went to college in Texas.

Brad: Did you get a job right after graduation?

Paula: No, I traveled for a while in Europe after college, and then I lived in France.

Brad: When was that?

Paula: Let's see… That was about six years ago.

Brad: I bet that was interesting. What did you do there?

Paula: I studied French. Anyway… that's enough about me. How about you? Were you born in L.A.?

1. GIVING AND GETTING PERSONAL INFORMATION (1)

✦ Where are you from?	✧ (I'm from) *Canada*, originally.
✦ Where were you born?	✧ (I was born in) *Montreal*.
✦ Were you born in | *Los Angeles?* *Hong Kong?*	✧ Yes, I was. No, | I was born in | *Canada*. I'm from

Practice

Ask your classmates where they were born. How many different cities did you find? Make a list.

2. GIVING AND GETTING PERSONAL INFORMATION (2)

✦ Did you *go to school* here?

✧ Yes. I *went to high school* here, but I *went to college in Texas*.
No. I *went to school in Boston*.

✦ Did you *get a job right after college*?

✧ No, I *traveled in Europe for awhile*.
Yes, I *started working right away*.

Practice 1

You and your partner are Brad and Paula. Brad asks and Paula answers. Use the cues below to make your questions and answers.
Follow this model:

Cue	**Question or Answer**
Brad: grow up in Los Angeles?	**Brad:** Did you grow up in L.A.?
Paula: No/Canada	**Paula:** No. I grew up in Canada.

Brad	**Paula**
1. go to high school here?	1. yes/high school in L.A.
2. go to college here?	2. no/college in Texas
3. travel after college?	3. yes/also lived in France
4. work in France?	4. no/studied French

Practice 2

Ask your partner these questions about his/her life. Ask more of your own, then reverse roles.

1. grow up around here?
2. study English in elementary school?
3. have teachers from the United States?

3. BEING SPECIFIC

✦ I *traveled in Europe for awhile.*

✧ Did you? And when was that?

✦ That was | *about six years ago.*
              in 1989.
              when I was twenty-one.
              right after college.

Practice 1

Look at the time line below. You and your partner are Brad and Paula. Paula will make statements about her life using the cues. Brad will ask when she did the things she talks about.
Follow the model. Then reverse roles. This time, Paula tells how many years ago she did things, or how old she was at the time.

Paula's cues
1. began school/Montreal
2. moved/L.A./high school
3. college/Texas
4. travel/Europe
5. study/France
6. first job/translator

Example
Paula: I began school in Montreal.
Brad: When was that?
Paula: That was in *1974.*
                That was *21 years ago.*
                That was when *I was six.*

Age:	6	14	18	21	22	24
	Dorval Elementary School	Kennedy High School, L.A.	University of Texas	Europe	France	First Job: Translation Services
Year:	1974	1982	1986	1989	1990	1992...1995
Years Ago:	21	13	9	6	5	3

Practice 2

Now think about yourself. Fill in the time line below and tell your partner about your life. He/she will ask when each event happened. Try to use all of the forms practiced.

When:				

LISTEN TO THIS

🔊 Now Brad is telling Paula about his life. As you listen, fill in the events in the time line for Brad. The first event is done for you.

When: *I was 2*	in 1960	I was 10	in 1972	after college
moved to Japan				

What activities from your childhood do you still enjoy today?

Are there any that you no longer enjoy?

Pronunciation Focus

Did you is pronounced [didya]. Listen and practice these sentences.

When did you change your mind?
How long did you stay there?
What did you do after that?

Now practice the conversation. Pay attention to *did you*.

John: Kathy! How are you? It's been ages! What are you doing these days?

Kathy: I just opened my own restaurant. I'm also head chef.

John: You're kidding! You've always hated cooking!

Kathy: Well, I used to hate cooking, but now I love it.

John: When did you change your mind?

Kathy: After I tried French food. Before that, I used to cook really boring things for my family.

John: I still can't believe it! So, did you go to cooking school or something?

Kathy: Yeah. I went to California to study.

John: Really? How long did you stay there?

Kathy: I was there between '88 and '90.

John: And what did you do after that?

Kathy: Then I came back here. I worked for about three years to get some experience.

John: That's great! So, where is your restaurant? I'm going to eat there this weekend!

1. DISCUSSING LENGTH OF TIME

✦ How long did you stay | *in California?*
                         | *there?*

✧ I | stayed | there | between *'92 and '94.*
   | was | | from *1992 to 1994.*
   | | | for *two years.*

KATHY SIMS

9/84.........Entered Lincoln High, Cleveland

6/88.........Graduated high school

6/88–9/88.........Summer job: Chef's helper

9/88.........Entered California School of Cooking

9/90.........Graduated with honors

9/90.........Returned to Cleveland

9/90–11/90.........Looking for work

12/90–1/91.........First job: Gaston's Restaurant

1/91–1/92.........Second job: Little Paris Cafe

1/92–12/92.........Third job: La Maison Restaurant

1/93.........Opened own restaurant

Practice 1

Look at Kathy's resume. Your partner is Kathy. Ask her how long she did these things. Kathy answers using all three forms above. Then reverse roles.

Student A asks:
1. go to Lincoln High
2. go to cooking school
3. look for work

Student B asks:
1. work as a chef's helper
2. live in California
3. work at Gaston's

Practice 2

Look at the time line that your partner did on page 75. Ask him/her about it, then reverse roles.

2. ASKING "WHAT NEXT?"

✦ What did you do | after you *left California?*
                  | after *leaving California?*
                  | after *that?*
                  | *then?*

✧ Well, then I *came back here.*

Practice 1

You are Kathy. Your partner will ask you about your education and work history, using the forms above. Then reverse roles.

Practice 2

Find a new partner. Look at the time line that he/she did on page 75. Ask him/her about it, then reverse roles.

3. DESCRIBING CHANGES

✦ I used to hate *cooking*, but now I love it.
I used to *cook really boring things* but now I don't.

Practice

Get into a small group. Tell the other group members three things that used to be true for you. Say how they have changed. Take turns.

LISTEN TO THIS

📼 You are going to hear a college literature teacher talking about Ernest Hemingway. Answer the questions below.

1. When did Hemingway write *The Sun Also Rises*?

....

2. What is the subject of *A Farewell to Arms?*

....

3. What was his occupation the second time he went to Europe?

....

4. When did he write *The Old Man and the Sea*?

....

5. Why was this short novel so powerful and emotional?

....

6. When did Hemingway kill himself?

....

(Student A looks at this page. Student B looks at the next page.)

Practice 1

Your partner is a career counselor who is helping you to write a new resume. Answer his/her questions.

Practice 2

You are a career counselor. You are helping your partner to write a new resume. If your partner has never worked before, get as much information as you can about his/her interests and hobbies. Complete the form below, look at it again, and suggest a new career for your partner.

RESUME WORKSHEET

Name: _____
Address: _____
Telephone: _____
Place of Birth: _____
Date of Birth: _____

Education

Name and Location	From Month/Year	To Month/Year	Degrees
High School			
College			
Other Education or Training			

Employment History

Name of Company	From Month/Year	To Month/Year	Duties

Activities, Interests, and Hobbies
(Please describe fully.)

_____
_____
_____
_____

PERSON TO PERSON — STUDENT **B**

(Student B looks at this page. Student A looks at the previous page.)

Practice 1

You are a career counselor. You are helping your partner to write a new resume. If your partner has never worked before, get as much information as you can about his/her interests and hobbies. Complete the form below, look at it again, and suggest a new career for your partner.

RESUME WORKSHEET

Name: _____
Address: _____
Telephone: _____
Place of Birth: _____
Date of Birth: _____

Education

Name and Location	From Month/Year	To Month/Year	Degrees
High School			
College			
Other Education or Training			

Employment History

Name of Company	From Month/Year	To Month/Year	Duties

Activities, Interests, and Hobbies
(Please describe fully.)

_____
_____
_____

Practice 2

Your partner is a career counselor who is helping you to write a new resume. Answer his/her questions.

CONVERSATION 1
HAVE YOU EVER BEEN TO JAPAN?

Where have you been on vacation?
How would you describe it to friends?

Jack: Have you ever been to Japan? I'm going in the fall.

Ted: Yeah, I've been there twice.

Jack: Really? Tell me about it. What's it like?

Ted: Oh, it's fantastic.

Jack: Where did you go?

Ted: On my first trip I went to Tokyo, and on my second trip I visited Kyoto.

Jack: What did you think of Tokyo?

Ted: Very big and exciting, but very crowded, too.

Jack: Yeah. I've seen pictures of the crowds!

Ted: And the restaurants are excellent... but they're kind of expensive.

Jack: And how about Kyoto?

Ted: Kyoto is lovely. It's full of beautiful old temples and gardens. It's a very historic city.

Jack: How was the weather?

Ted: I was in Tokyo in August, and it was really hot and humid. I went to Kyoto in October. It was hot and sunny, but there was no humidity.

Jack: Sounds perfect. I can't wait!

1. ASKING ABOUT PAST EXPERIENCES

✦ Have you ever been to *Japan?*

✧ Yes. | (I've been there) *twice.*   ✧ No, never.
       | I was there *last summer.*

Practice 1

Combine a verb in the first column with an appropriate phrase from the second column and form a question like the example. (You may combine some verbs with several phrases.) Student A asks Student B four questions. Student B answers truthfully. Then reverse roles.

Example:
Have you ever been to a rock concert?

been to ————————————→ apple cider

eaten   a rock concert

tried   a wrestling match

seen   snow

visited   Disneyland

gone to   a foreign country

made   Mexican food

had   a surprise party

Practice 2

Think of three more ideas of your own. Ask your partner and two other classmates.

2. ASKING FOR A DESCRIPTION OR OPINION

✦ What | did | you think of | *Tokyo?*
       | do | | *it?*

  How was | *Tokyo?*
          | *it?*

  What | was | *Tokyo* | like?
       | is | *it* |

✧ It was *very big* and *exciting,* but it was very *crowded.*
  It's *quite old,* but *it has a lot of modern buildings.*

✦ What | was | the *weather* like?
       | is |

  How | was | the *weather?*
      | is |

✧ It was *really hot and humid.*

First choose a town or city to talk about. Your partner will ask you to discuss these and other similar topics. To answer, use words from the box and words of your own. Then reverse roles.

Example:
Let's talk about Chicago. What's the downtown area like?

the downtown area
the hotels
the restaurants
the public transportation
the weather
the stores
the food
the people

well-kept	attractive
small	inefficient
clean	expensive
big	uncomfortable
cheap	run-down
crowded	noisy
quiet	exciting
humid	rainy
spicy	boring
dry	inexpensive
cold	kind

LISTEN TO THIS

 Minako has just come back from a vacation in San Francisco. She is telling her friend Lin about it. Listen and write down Minako's opinions on the following. One or two words are enough.

San Francisco .... restaurants ....

transportation .... hotel ....

Think of two cities you have visited.
Which one did you like better? Why?

Dana: Oh, hi Pam. When did you get back from Canada? How was it?

Pam: The day before yesterday. I only visited Montreal and Ottawa, but I had a great time.

Dana: Which city did you like better?

Pam: That's hard to say... I think Ottawa is prettier. It has better sightseeing, too. A lot of museums and galleries.

Dana: And what's Montreal like? What did you think of it?

Pam: Montreal is more exciting. It has better shopping. The stores are cheaper and more interesting.

Dana: Which one has better nightlife?

Pam: Oh, Montreal for sure. It has more restaurants and clubs. They say Montreal is the most exciting city in Canada.

Dana: Well, I've always wanted to see Vancouver. I've heard it has the most beautiful views.

Pronunciation Focus

Wh- questions have falling intonation. Listen and practice these questions.

When did you get back from Canada?↘

Which city did you like better?↘

What did you think of it?↘

Which one has better nightlife?↘

Now practice the conversation. Pay attention to intonation.

1. COMPARING PLACES (1)

✦ What's | Montreal | like?
      | Ottawa |

✧ It's *more exciting* than *Ottawa*.
   It's *prettier* than *Montreal*.

Practice

As a class or in a small group, choose two cities and compare them. Make statements using these words.

older	more expensive
newer	more interesting
busier	more attractive
quieter	more exciting
cleaner	more crowded

2. COMPARING PLACES (2)

✦ Which city has | *more interesting* | *sightseeing?*
        | *better* | *shopping?*

✧ *Ottawa*. There are more *museums*.
   Montreal. The *stores* are more *interesting*.

Practice

Think of a city or area that you have visited. Your partner will ask you to compare it to your hometown. Give reasons for your comparisons. Think of more questions of your own. Then reverse roles.

Ask which has:

1. nicer weather
2. newer buildings
3. cheaper restaurants
4. bigger hotels

5. better sightseeing
6. older neighborhoods
7. better public transportation
8. friendlier people

3. COMPARING PLACES (3)

> ✦ Which *city* is the most *exciting*?
> ✧ *Montreal* is the most *exciting city in Canada.*
>
> ✦ Which *city* has the *best scenery*?
> ✧ *Vancouver.* It has the most *beautiful views in Canada.*

Practice 1

You want to find out what people think is best about your city. With a partner, on a separate piece of paper, write four questions. You need two questions for each of the models above. Ask other classmates for their opinions and write down their answers.

Examples:
Which shopping area is best?
Which restaurant has the best food?

Practice 2

With your partner, look at the answers. Then discuss the results with the class.

LISTEN TO THIS

▭ Susan is going on a business trip to Boston. She is asking her secretary, Elaine, about hotels there. Listen and fill in the chart below.

	The Midtown	The Boston Bay	The Fairfield
Best location			
Newest			
Most expensive			
Cheapest			
Best restaurant			

PERSON TO PERSON

STUDENT A

(Student A looks at this page. Student B looks at the next page.)

▭ Bob and Ruth have just returned from Europe. You are going to hear their opinions about Paris, London, and Rome.

Practice 1

Before you listen, check whether you think London or Paris is noisier, has worse traffic, and so, on. Use the boxes below.

Practice 2

Now listen to Bob's opinions about London and Paris, and check the appropriate box.

		Your opinion			Bob's opinion	
		London	Paris		London	Paris
Worse traffic						
Noisier						
Better art galleries						
More interesting restaurants						
Better nightlife						

Practice 3

Compare all four opinions: yours, your partner's, Bob's, and Ruth's.

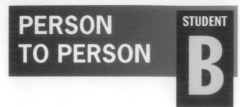

PERSON TO PERSON — STUDENT B

(Student B looks at this page. Student A looks at the previous page.)

Bob and Ruth have just returned from Europe. You are going to hear their opinions about Paris, London, and Rome.

Practice 1

Before you listen, check whether you think Paris or Rome is noisier, has worse traffic, and so on. Use the boxes below.

Practice 2

Now listen to Ruth's opinions about Paris and Rome, and check the appropriate box.

👍👎	Your opinion			Ruth's opinion	
	Paris	Rome		Paris	Rome
Worse traffic					
Noisier					
Better art galleries					
More interesting restaurants					
Better nightlife					

Practice 3

Compare all four opinions: yours, your partner's, Bob's, and Ruth's.

What plans do you have for the future?
Are you going to graduate soon? Get a job? Get married? Travel?

Counselor: Only three more months to go! So, what are you going to do after you graduate, Donna?

Donna: I'm going to go to college in Ohio.

Counselor: Have you decided what you're going to major in?

Donna: Uh-huh. I'm planning to study engineering.

Counselor: That's a good field. And what about you, Simon?

Simon: My father is going to give me a job in his company. I'll probably work there about a year so I can learn the basics.

Counselor: And what are you doing after that?

Simon: After that I'm going back to school to get my degree in business.

Counselor: That sounds very practical. How about you, Fong? What do you plan to do next year?

Fong: I'm planning to take it easy for a while. I'm going to spend some time traveling in Europe, but I'm coming back after that to study.

Counselor: How long will you be there?

Fong: Well, I'm leaving in June, and I'm coming home for Christmas, so I'll be there about six months.

1. DISCUSSING FUTURE PLANS (1)

✦ What do you What are you	plan to going to planning to	do	after you graduate? in the fall? next year?

✧ I'm	going to planning to	go to college. take it easy.	✧ I don't know yet. I haven't decided yet.

Practice

Find a partner. Take turns asking each other about future plans. Use the cues below to ask. Then add two questions of your own.

1. after you finish this class
2. after school/work tonight
3. for your next vacation
4. the day after tomorrow
5. this weekend
6. on Friday night

2. DISCUSSING FUTURE PLANS (2)

✦ What are you doing after that?

✧ I'm	going back to school after that. working for my father next year.	✧ I'm not sure yet. I'm still not sure.

Practice 1

Student A: Ask your partner what he/she is doing at the following times.
Student B: Answer using one of the choices below.

Student A	Student B
1. next summer	1. visit California relax and take it easy get a part-time job
2. on the weekend	2. go to the beach stay home have friends over for dinner
3. for your birthday	3. have a small party go out to a nice restaurant not do anything special
4. on New Year's Eve	4. go to a dance watch TV go to a party

Practice 2

Repeat Practice 1, but this time answer using your own plans. Think of other times to ask about. Then reverse roles.

3. DISCUSSING FUTURE PLANS (3)

✦ How long will you be there?
✧ I'll be there *for about six months.*

✦ When will you be *in Chicago?*
✧ I'll be there │ *a week from today.*
  │ *on the sixteenth.*

✦ Where will you be │ *at six o'clock?*
  │ *on Sunday afternoon?*
✧ I'll be *at home.*

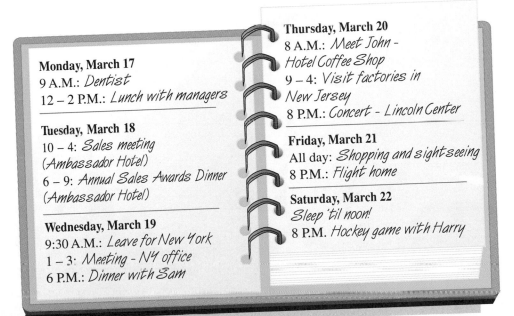

Monday, March 17
9 A.M.: *Dentist*
12 – 2 P.M.: *Lunch with managers*

Tuesday, March 18
10 – 4: *Sales meeting*
(Ambassador Hotel)
6 – 9: *Annual Sales Awards Dinner*
(Ambassador Hotel)

Wednesday, March 19
9:30 A.M.: *Leave for New York*
1 – 3: *Meeting - NY office*
6 P.M.: *Dinner with Sam*

Thursday, March 20
8 A.M.: *Meet John -*
Hotel Coffee Shop
9 – 4: *Visit factories in*
New Jersey
8 P.M.: *Concert - Lincoln Center*

Friday, March 21
All day: *Shopping and sightseeing*
8 P.M.: *Flight home*

Saturday, March 22
Sleep 'til noon!
8 P.M. *Hockey game with Harry*

Practice

Look at your appointment book for next week and answer your partner's questions. Your partner will ask you:

1. three *when* questions
2. three *where* questions
3. three *how long* questions

Then reverse roles.

LISTEN TO THIS

Irene Reynolds is the busy president of a large company. Listen as Jim, the assistant, gives Irene her schedule for Monday of next week. Fill in her appointment book.

MONDAY

APPOINTMENTS & EVENTS			
Hours	Appointment	Hours	Appointment
8:00 am		4:00 pm	
9:00 am		5:00 pm	
10:00 am		6:00 pm	
11:00 am		7:00 pm	
12:00 pm		8:00 pm	
1:00 pm		9:00 pm	
2:00 pm		10:00 pm	
3:00 pm		11:00 pm	

What is a New Year's resolution?
Have you ever made one?
What are some typical resolutions?

Pronunciation Focus

The stressed words in a sentence usually have a regular beat. Listen and practice.

I'd like to lóse some wéight.

I wánt to sáve some móney.

Whát are you góing to dó?

Whére do you thínk you'll gó?

Now practice the conversation. Try to give stressed words a regular beat.

Henry: Hi, Alice . . . have you made any New Year's resolutions yet?

Alice: Just the usual. I'd like to lose some weight, and I want to save some money.

Henry: Come on! Everybody makes those resolutions!

Alice: I know. Well, I hope I'll get a promotion at work, but that's not a resolution. I am going to work harder. How about you?

Henry: Hmm, I quit smoking last June. That was last year's promise to myself.

Alice: So, what do you want to do this year?

Henry: I want to start getting more exercise. I have to lose weight, so I'd like to join a health club. Jeff . . . what are you going to do?

Jeff: I'd like to treat myself to a really nice vacation.

Alice: Oh? Where do you think you'll go?

Jeff: I don't know. I might go to a quiet beach in Mexico, or I might go fishing up in Canada. I haven't made up my mind yet.

1. DISCUSSING THE FUTURE

✦ What do you want to do?
What would you like to do?
What are you going to do?

✧ I'd like to | *lose some weight.*
I want to | *start getting more exercise.*

Practice

Make three New Year's resolutions. Your partner will ask you what they are. Choose from the list below or make up your own. Your partner will ask you for more information. Then reverse roles.

learn to play an instrument   get better grades

keep a diary   study more

read a book a month   take up a new hobby

2. DISCUSSING HOPES

✦ What do you hope | will happen?
you'll do?
to do?

✧ I hope | *I'll get a promotion.*
I get a promotion.
to get a promotion.

Practice 1

Form a small group to discuss your future goals. Ask and answer like this:

Student A: What do you hope to do in the next five years?
Student B: I hope to travel.

Practice 2

Repeat Practice 1, but this time ask about the next ten years.

3. DISCUSSING POSSIBILITIES

✦ *Where* do you think you'll *go*? *Where* are you going to *go*?	
✧ I might | *go to Mexico.* *go fishing in Canada.*	✧ I haven't made up my mind yet.

Practice 1

With your partner, discuss some possible choices for future plans. Answer each other's questions freely and reverse roles as you go along. Follow the example below.

Cue: college/apply to after high school
Question: Which college do you think you'll apply to after high school?

1. which subject/major in at university
2. which company/apply to after college
3. where/go on your vacation
4. when/take your vacation
5. how long/be in Europe
6. who/marry

Practice 2

Think of some more questions about the future to discuss with your partner. Try to use *which, where, when, who,* and *how long.*

LISTEN TO THIS

▭ Alessandro is talking to his friend about what he wants to do this summer. He mentions all of the things below. Listen and put a question mark (**?**) beside the things he might do or wants to do. Put a check (✔) beside the things he will definitely do.

..........work in his father's restaurant

..........save money

..........take time off

..........read

..........rent movies

..........go to a friend's cabin

..........go waterskiing and swimming

..........help build a dock

..........visit uncle in Italy

..........go to Milan

..........go to Florence

..........move to a new apartment

..........organize new apartment

(Student A looks at this page. Student B looks at the next page.)

▭ Ben and Jill are high school friends who will be graduating soon. They are talking to each other about the future.

Practice 1

Listen and take short notes on Ben's future hopes and plans. Jill's are given to you.

	BEN	JILL
After high school		• *go to Harvard* • *major in Business and Economics*
After college		• *go to law school* • *practice law*
Future hopes		• *go into politics* • *make a lot of money* • *be president of the U.S.*

Practice 2

Check your answers with your partner's information.

Look at the information about Ben and Jill again and decide which of them you are more similar to. If you are more like Jill, put an X close to her name. If you are more like Ben, put an X close to his name.

More like Jill		More like Ben

Practice 3

Compare your X with your partner's. Start your discussion of the reasons like this: "I think I'm more like Jill/Ben because..."

(Student B looks at this page. Student A looks at the previous page.)

Ben and Jill are high school friends who will be graduating soon. They are talking to each other about the future.

Practice 1

Listen and take short notes on Jill's future hopes and plans. Ben's are given to you.

	JILL	BEN
After high school		• work for Dad for a year • go to college • study literature or art
After college		• easy job • 9 to 5
Future hopes		• steady job • nice family

Practice 2

Check your answers with your partner's information.

Look at the information about Ben and Jill again and decide which of them you are more similar to. If you are more like Jill, put an X close to her name. If you are more like Ben, put an X close to his name.

More like Jill		More like Ben

Practice 3

Compare your X with your partner's. Start your discussion of the reasons like this: "I think I'm more like Jill/Ben because..."

LET'S TALK

Once every three years, the government does a survey about people and their occupations. Interview a classmate, and fill out the form below. Then find a new partner and reverse roles.

If you and your classmates are students, make up an occupation and employer that you think is interesting.

Start like this: "Could I ask you a few questions, please?"

SURVEY

NAME _____
            Last   *First*

ADDRESS _____

_____

_____

_____

TELEPHONE _____
               Area Code   *Number*

OCCUPATION _____

EMPLOYER _____

Someone you know is going to win an award today. You know who it is, but you can't tell anyone. However, the other members of your group might be able to guess from a description.

Get into groups of four people. Each member of the group thinks of a person who is well-known to all the other group members: a teacher? another student? a co-worker? Fill in one column of the chart below, but don't show it to anyone. The other group members will ask for information and fill in their charts. Then they will guess who you are describing. Take turns.

Start like this: "I can't tell you who it is, but I can answer questions."

Your names:				
Descriptions:				
Sex				
Age				
Height				
Weight				
Hair color				
Hair length				
Hair style				
Other details				
Person's name				

You and your partner are interior design students. Your homework is to decorate and furnish a one-bedroom apartment. Remember to think about sizes, shapes, and colors. This will be a model apartment, so you have to pay attention to details.

Start like this: "Which room do you want to talk about first?"

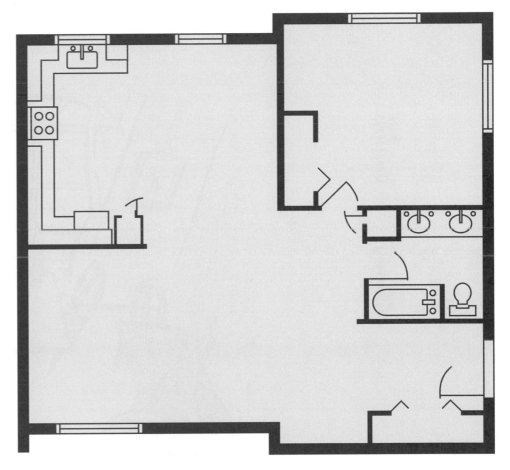

Situation:

You have just moved to a new city, and you don't know anybody. However, your cousin gave you the name and phone number of a friend. Call the friend, chat, and agree to meet.

Be sure to tell your partner what you look like. End the conversation by saying something like "Let's meet at the Cafe Coco. I'll be at the table in..."

With your partner, write the telephone conversation. Look at Units 1, 2, and 3 to help you. Then join another pair of students and perform your conversation.

Start like this: "This is .... speaking. My cousin gave me your number and said I should call you..."

A group of six foreign students is coming to your city on an exchange program. You have been asked to plan their schedule for three days.

With a partner, decide where you want to take them, and when. Remember to think about when restaurants, stores, clubs, and sightseeing places open and close. Also, think about locations. Everyone will be walking or using public transportation.

Here is some information to help you plan.
- There are three male and three female students.
- They are all between 17 and 19 years of age.
- They are all staying in a college dormitory nearby.
- They get breakfast at the dorm, but not lunch or dinner.
- They asked for some free time.

Start like this: "Let's think of as many places as we can. Then we can choose some and arrange the schedule."

Itinerary

Day One	Day Two	Day Three

You and your partner are going on vacation for ten days. Try to reach an agreement about where you will go and what you will do. Discuss the things you like and dislike with your partner.

What things are there to do and see in these places?

Can you think of any that are not in the posters?

Start like this: "I like big cities. How about you?"

You and your partner enjoy each other's company, so you want to spend some time together outside of class.

Student A: Think of a place or activity that you like. Then, think of a time when you are free, and invite your partner.

Student B: Consider your partner's invitation. Do you like his/her suggestion? Are you free at that time? Do you want to change or add to the invitation? Decide on a plan that is good for both of you, and make all your final arrangements.

Start like this: "We should get together some time. What do you like doing outside of class?"

Situation:

Your school/company is having a "Getting To Know You" party. You want to find someone who likes some of the same things you do, and arrange to do them together.

Approach a classmate you don't know well. Introduce yourself and try to find activities you both like. If you find something, arrange a time and a place to meet and give directions to the place. If you can't find something you both like to do, approach another classmate. Look at Units 4, 5, and 6 for help or ideas.

Start like this: "Hi. This party is a great idea, isn't it? I'm .... , and I really like .... "

Anne-Marie is getting married, and you and your friends want to buy her a nice gift. You have enough money to get one of the choices below.
Get into a group of four people and compare the items below. If you have another idea, suggest it. Then, as a group, make a final decision about which gift you want to buy for her. Be sure to give reasons.

Start like this: "Which one of these gifts do you think is best?"

You and your partner are going to open a restaurant in San Diego, California. Plan your new restaurant.

Start like this: "What kind of food do you think we should serve?"

Type of food: ....

Size of restaurant: ....

Decor: ....

After you decide on the decor, the size of the restaurant, and the type of food you want to serve, plan your menu—including prices.

MENU

You are a college student. You were away visiting friends for the weekend. When you left on Friday afternoon, your apartment was spotless. When you got home on Friday evening, this is how you found the apartment and your roommate. Complain politely to your partner, and request action.

Start like this: "I hate to mention it, but look at this apartment!"

Situation 1:

Student A: You are a very fussy shopper. Nothing is ever 'just right.' Decide on an item to buy. See Units 7 and 9 for help and ideas.

Start like this: "Can you help me? I'm looking for a/an ...., but I can't find one that I really like."

Student B: You are the sales clerk who is helping Student A.

Situation 2:

Reverse roles.

Student A: You are a new waiter/waitress. Your partner will use a menu from Unit 8 to place his/her order. Use Unit 9 also, for more ideas and helpful language.

Student B: You are a very fussy customer. Nothing that you are served is ever 'just right.' Use the menu from Unit 8 to place your order. Also use Unit 9 for more ideas and helpful language. Then role-play the conversation with your partner.

Start like this: "Excuse me! I'm sorry, but I can't possibly eat/drink these things. First of all, . . . "

Imagine that you are a famous person, real or fictional. Your partner is a screenwriter who wants to make a movie about you. He/she is going to interview you about your life. (You don't have to know anything about the person you choose. Have fun making up the details.)

Your partner uses the chart below to write down your answers. Then reverse roles.

Start like this: "Before I can write this movie, I have to ask you a few questions about your life. First of all, . . . "

When:	What happened:

Get into a small group and exchange opinions with your classmates. Discuss what each of you *thinks* is the correct answer to these questions. Give reasons wherever possible.

What do you think is:

1. the best country to go to on vacation?
2. the worst country to go to on vacation?
3. the most dangerous city in (your country)?
4. the most dangerous city in the world?
5. the hottest country in the world?
6. the most interesting historical location in your country?
7. the most expensive country to visit?
8. the cheapest country to go to on vacation?

Start like this: "What do you think is the largest country in the world?"

A wealthy stranger has died and left you and your partner half a million dollars each – for your personal use. But. . . there's a catch. In order to get your money the two of you must spend two million dollars of the stranger's money to improve life in your community. Decide how the money will be spent. After the two of you make your final decision, discuss how each of you is going to spend your half million.

Use the chart below. (It isn't necessary to use all six spaces.)

Start like this: "What things would make our community better?"

COMMUNITY IMPROVEMENTS

AMOUNT:	PROJECT:

Situation:

People can learn from their own experiences. They can also learn from other people's experiences. Talk with your classmates about experiences.

Get into a small group and talk about an interesting or important experience you have had. Your classmates will ask you questions to get more details. Did anyone's experience give you an idea about something you want to do in the future? Talk about that, too. Check Units 10, 11, and 12 for help.

Start like this: "When I was young, I had a very funny/embarrassing/frightening/important experience. This is what happened . . ."

TAPESCRIPT

Conversation 1
Man:	Great wedding, isn't it? Are you a friend of the bride or the groom?
Woman:	The bride. We went to college together.
Man:	Really? I work with the groom. Oh, by the way, my name's Bob...Bob Bradley.
Woman:	Hi, Bob. I'm June Owens.
Man:	I'm sorry. I didn't get your first name.
Woman:	It's June. Nice to meet you.
Man:	You, too. So, what do you do, June?
Woman:	I'm a teller at the Bank of New York. How about you?
Man:	I'm a computer programmer.

Conversation 2
Man:	Tim always has good parties, doesn't he?
Woman:	He sure does! Do you go to school with Tim?
Man:	Yeah. We study law together at Princeton University. How about you?
Woman:	I'm in the Fine Arts program at Smith College. My name's Kim Jackson, by the way.
Man:	Nice to meet you, Kim. I'm John Hunt.
Woman:	Well, John...would you like to dance?
Man:	I'd love to.

Conversation 3
Woman:	What did you think of the speeches?
Man:	I learned a lot about international business.
Woman:	Is this your first conference?
Man:	Yes, it is. It's very nice to meet you. I'm Mario Pirelli. Please call me Mario.
Woman:	Okay...Mario. My name's Mayumi Yamada.
Man:	I'm sorry. I didn't catch your first name.
Woman:	It's Mayumi. What company do you work for, Mario?
Man:	I'm with Coca-Cola. How about you?
Woman:	I work for the Sony Corporation.

Jean:	I'd like to apply for a credit card.
Mr. Ames:	All right. Please have a seat. Now...are you a regular customer at Darcy's Department Store?
Jean:	Oh, yes. I love this store. I shop here all the time.
Mr. Ames:	That's good. OK. Could I have your name, please?
Jean:	Jean Sands.
Mr. Ames:	How do you spell your first name?
Jean:	It's J-E-A-N.
Mr. Ames:	Thank you. And where do you live?
Jean:	30 Jackson Street.
Mr. Ames:	I'm sorry. Did you say 13 or 30?
Jean:	30. Three zero.
Mr. Ames:	Is that in Boston?
Jean:	No, it's in Salem. The zip code is 01970.
Mr. Ames:	I also need your telephone number.
Jean:	It's 654-1315. (thirteen fifteen)
Mr. Ames:	And what's your occupation?
Jean:	I'm a chef at the Bayside Hotel.
Mr. Ames:	Chef at the Bayside Hotel? All right. One more thing...do you have a local bank account?
Jean:	Yes, I do...at East National Bank.
Mr. Ames:	OK, Ms. Sands. I think that's everything. You'll receive your card in about a month.
Jean:	Thank you very much.

Officer:	Next please. Good afternoon, sir. May I have your disembarkation card?
Male:	What?
Officer:	Your landing card. Do you have one?
Male:	No. I have no card.
Officer:	Well, I'm afraid you need one. Here, let me help you. First of all, could I have your surname please?
Male :	My name?
Officer:	Yes...Your surname...last name...your family name.
Male :	Ah, yes. Of course. It's Rosenzweig. R-O-S-E-N-Z-W-E-I-G.
Officer:	R-O-S-E-N-Z-W-E-I-G. Thank you. And your first name?
Male:	Albrecht.
Officer:	I'm sorry, but you're going to have to spell that one, too.
Male :	A-L-B-R-E-C-H-T.
Officer:	All right. And what's your occupation, Mr. Rosenzweig? What do you do?
Male :	I'm a businessman.
Officer:	And when were you born? What's your birthday?
Male :	17 June, 1945.
Officer:	June 17, 1945. And your nationality?
Male :	My country? ...Austria.
Officer:	So, you're Austrian. And are you here on business or pleasure?
Male :	I'm sorry?
Officer:	What is the reason for your trip? Why did you come to the United States?
Male :	Why? To visit my brother.
Officer:	Fine. And where will you be staying?
Male:	With my brother, of course.
Officer:	All right. What's his address, please? Where does he live?
Male :	238 East 82nd Street, New York, New York.
Officer:	238 East 82nd Street. OK, that's it. Thank you and have a nice stay.

1. This is me and my oldest son, Ted, with my two little granddaughters. They're twins, you know...just three years old. They were really excited when the cake came in. Of course, they had to help me blow out the candles!

2. Now, this man, this is my nephew. He played the piano when they sang "Happy Birthday". We're very proud of him. He's only 19 and he plays with the City Symphony Orchestra. That's his father, my youngest brother, standing behind him.

3. And this is my husband, Sam, with our youngest son. He's twenty-one and is in his last year of college. He wants to go to law school next year. I'm sure he'll make it. He's a straight-A student you know. Smart...just like his mother!

4. Here's the last one. This is my other brother with my nieces. The older girl is seventeen, and the younger one is fifteen, so they're both still in high school. It's impossible to call my brother because one of those girls is always on the phone!

Detective: OK. So everyone here actually *saw* the man riding his motorcycle through the flower beds at City Hall?

Chorus of Voices: Oh, yes! I did! I saw him!

Detective: Quiet, please! I can't listen to everyone talking at the same time! Thank you. I'll speak to each of you, alone, in my office.

Conversation 1
Detective: What did he look like?
Witness 1: Well, let me see...I think he was short, and very thin. He had, umm, light brown hair.
Detective: And what was his hair like?
Witness 1: It was medium length and curly.
Detective: Age?
Witness 1: I guess...early thirties.
Detective: So, he was between thirty-one and thirty-three years old?
Witness 1: Yes, that's right.
Detective: One more question. Do you remember what he was wearing?
Witness 1: He had on a blue and red golf shirt, shorts, and knee socks.
Detective: Well, thank you for coming in.
Witness 1: You're welcome.

Conversation 2
Detective: First of all, thank you for waiting.
Witness 2: Oh, no problem. I like to help the police when I can.
Detective: Fine. Now, what did the man look like?

Witness 2: He was pretty tall and thin. I think he was about twenty.
Detective: Good. And what about his hair? What was it like?
Witness 2: Oh. It was wavy and kind of short. It was blond or brown... Wait. It was blond.
Detective: And what about his clothes?
Witness 2: Tsk. Terrible. Not fashionable at all!
Detective: I mean...what did he have on?
Witness 2: Well. He was wearing a blue golf shirt with red stripes, and a pair of brown shorts. *And* he had on black socks. Can you believe it? Red *and* blue *and* brown *and* black? Terrible.
Detective: OK. That's everything. Thanks again, and could you send in the next person, please?

Conversation 3
Detective: Come in please, and have a seat. So, can you describe the man for me?
Witness 3: OK. What do you want to know?
Detective: Let's start with clothes. What was he wearing?
Witness 3: Hmmm...Hmmm. I *think* it was a blue shirt.
Detective: Anything else?
Witness 3: Maybe... brown pants.
Detective: How about height? How tall was he?
Witness 3: I'm pretty sure he was tall, but he was sitting down. I remember he was pretty thin. And his hair...his hair was brown and curly. It was about medium-length.
Detective: Just one more question. His age...about how old was he?
Witness 3: I guess he was a teenager. In his late teens. He looked kind of young.
Detective: OK. Thank you for the information. I'm sure we'll catch him soon.

Conversation A
A: Hey Margo! Do you know where the scissors are?
B: Aren't they in the desk drawer?
A: No. That's the first place I looked.
B: Oh, I know. I was using them in the kitchen. Try beside the telephone.
A: Oh, yeah. I've got them. Thanks.

Conversation B
A: Mom...Do we have any ginger ale?
B: Yes. It's in the fridge.
A: No it isn't. Where in the fridge?
B: Look on the bottom shelf behind the juice.
A: Oh, I see it. Thanks.

Conversation C
A: What are you looking for?
B: My book. I can't find my book. Do you know where it is?
A: I saw it on the coffee table this morning.
B: You're right. Here it is. It was under the newspaper.

Conversation D

A: Excuse me. Do you sell computer disks?
B: Oh, yes. We sell all types of disks.
A: Great. And where do you keep them?
B: Do you see the computer section?
A: Uh-huh. Over there?
B: That's right. They're all on the middle shelf between the paper and the computer games.
A: I found them! Thanks for your help.

Speaker 1

Mine was the greatest invention ever! It's old, but people still need it today. It's round, and it comes in many sizes. Long ago, it was made of stone. It's also been made of wood. Then, people made it out of metal. Now, it's often made of rubber. It's used on cars, bicycles, and in machines.

Speaker 2

Well, my invention is more recent. It's long, narrow, and has a sharp point. It's usually made of plastic, but you can get expensive ones made of gold or silver. Everybody uses it. It's full of something called ink, and you write with it.

Speaker 3

The thing I invented has changed many times. Before, it was usually a wooden box with a big piece of ice in it. These days, it's a pretty big, rectangular box made of metal, and it has one or two doors. We have electricity now, so we don't need the ice. My invention keeps food cold or frozen.

Speaker 4

To tell you the truth, my invention isn't as important as those three, but it's still useful. My invention can be made of cotton, wool, silk, leather, or rubber. They're small, but they come in different sizes. You put them on your hands. Sometimes, they're used for fashion. But usually they're used to keep your hands warm, or to protect your hands when you work.

Speaker 5

My invention is very old. People use it to sweep their floors and keep them clean. Every house has one in it. It's very long and narrow. One end is much wider, and is usually made of straw.

Speaker 6

My invention is the newest. It's flat and round and has a very small hole right in the middle of it. It's quite small. In fact, it's usually smaller than your hand! You put it in a special machine and you can listen to music on it.

Speaker 7

You know, I'm very proud of my invention. I think it changed the world!
There are several in every house. They're also used outside. Now, they come in many sizes and colors, but they're always very small. They're usually round like a ball on top, and narrow at the bottom. My invention is made of glass and metal. People use them for light when it's dark.

Speaker 8

If you live in a cold place, you love my invention...especially at night. They're flat and usually square or rectangular. They're pretty big. Mostly, they're made of wool, but they can be made of cotton. You put one on your bed and it keeps you warm at night.

Ron: Well, Bruce. We're lucky we don't have to buy a whole lot of furniture.
Bruce: You're not kidding! So Ron, tell me what kind of stuff we're getting from your parents.
Ron: I think the best thing is probably the brown leather sofa. It's old, but it's in pretty good condition. Four people can sit on it comfortably.
Bruce: Fantastic.
Ron: They also gave us a wall unit. It's made of wood.
Bruce: How big is the wall unit?
Ron: It's tall, but it's not very long.
Bruce: Perfect! This summer I saved some extra money and bought a new CD player and some good speakers.
Ron: What size are the speakers?
Bruce: They're pretty small, but they sound great.
Ron: My mom also gave us two orange easy chairs. They're very wide and comfortable. They'll be perfect for studying.
Bruce: Yeah. Or for watching TV. My father said I could bring the old TV from home. It works well, and it has a big screen.
Ron: That's great! Our apartment is gonna be perfect.
Bruce: Really! I'm also bringing a glass coffee table and a floor lamp with a round shade.
Ron: Oh, good. Well, I also have two narrow lamps with square shades.
Bruce: I guess all we have to do now is decide where to put everything.

Conversation 1

A: City park swimming pool. Good morning.
B: Good morning. Could you tell me if the pool is open today?
A: Yes. The pool opens at 10:00 AM.
B: Oh, good. And what time does it close?
A: We have our summer hours now, so we close at 10:00 PM.
B: OK. Thank you very much.
A: You're quite welcome.

Conversation 2

A recorded voice says:
Hello. Thank you for calling The Golden Cinema Theater. Our specialty is movies from the good old days. Tonight we have two movies. The first is *Casablanca,* with Humphrey Bogart and Ingrid Bergman. It starts at 7:15 and ends at 9:00. Our second feature is *Breakfast at Tiffany's,* starring Audrey Hepburn. It starts at 9:30 and ends at 11:30. The admission price for members is $5.00, and $7.50 for non-members. Doors open at 6:45.

Conversation 3

A: Madison Square Garden. Can I help you?
B: Yes. Do you have any more tickets for the concert on Friday night?
A: Do you mean the Rock 'n' Roll Revival show? Yes, we still have some $25.00 tickets left.
B: Great. OK, and is the box office open now?
A: Yes, the box office is open from 10:00 to 8:00.
B: Oh, by the way, what time does the show start?
A: It starts at 8:00.
B: And what time does it end?
A: Well, there are four bands, so it'll probably end about midnight.
B: Thanks a lot.
A: No problem.

LISTEN TO THIS UNIT 4/PAGE 30

Location 1

A: It's about a five-minute walk from here. It's on Fourth Avenue, just past the post office.
B: So I walk up this street?
A: That's right. It's at the end of the third block, on the corner, across from the Sportsmen's Hotel.
B: I've got it. Thanks.
A: No problem.

Location 2

A: Just walk up Fourth one block to Twentieth Street. Turn left and walk one block to Third Avenue. Go up two more blocks, and you'll see it on the left, across from the day-care center.
B: Let me see... up Fourth to Twentieth, left on Twentieth to Third, up Third about two blocks. It's on the left side of the street?
A: That's it. Just past the park.
B: Great. Thanks for your help.
A: Sure.

Location 3

A: Go up this street and take the second right — that's at Twenty-First Street. Stay on the right side of the street. It's in the middle of that block, between the hardware store and the men's shop.
B: OK...so I want the second right, and it's in the middle of that block between what and what?
A: Between the hardware store — I think it's called Mel's — and a menswear place. You can't miss it.
B: I'm sure I'll find it. Thanks a lot.
A: OK.

Location 4

A: I'm sorry, but I don't know. We're not from around here.
B: Well, thanks anyway.
C: Wait! I saw it when we came out of that restaurant beside the hotel. Do you know the Tenth Inning Bar and Grill?
B: No, I don't.
C: It's easy. You walk up this street three blocks and turn right. Walk over one more block. You'll be at the corner of Fifth and Twenty-Second. You'll see it on Fifth Avenue, on the other corner across the street from the Tenth Inning.

B: So, I have to get to the corner of Fifth and Twenty-Second, and it'll be on my right?
C: Uh-huh. Across from the restaurant.
B: Thank you.
C: My pleasure. I'm always happy to help another tourist.

LISTEN TO THIS UNIT 5/PAGE 35

Stan: Thanks for coming out with me tonight.
Mary: Thanks for asking!
Stan: So. Dinner first. We could go out for a nice Chinese meal. I love the food at the Golden Dragon!
Mary: Oh, Stan. I don't really like Chinese food. I really just want a hamburger and french fries.
Stan: Oh, I see. I guess a hamburger and french fries will be OK tonight.
Mary: What do you want to do after dinner? There's a new musical at the State Street Cinema. I really love musicals.
Stan: Sorry, Mary. I hate musicals. But, you know...I want to see the documentary at the Triplex Theater. Do you like documentaries?
Mary: Documentaries usually put me to sleep. I can't stand them. Hmmm. Well, I have one more idea. We can go bowling. I like to bowl.
Stan: That *is* a good idea! I like bowling, too.

LISTEN TO THIS UNIT 5/PAGE 38

Conversation 1

A: Do you know why I love Sundays?
B: Sure. You don't work today.
A: That's true, but also, there are sports on TV all day.
B: Oh...yeah.
A: So... What do you want to watch? Football? Basketball? Golf? Which one do you like?
B: To be honest, I don't really like watching sports. Maybe I'll read.

Conversation 2

A: Do you know any good places for dinner around here? I want to go somewhere new and different.
B: Well, I really like the Cafe Pronto. They have fantastic Italian food.
A: Do they? I love Italian food! Is it very expensive there?
B: That's another good thing about it. It's not expensive at all.
A: Sounds perfect.

Conversation 3

A: This book is just excellent. I'm really enjoying it.
B: What is it?
A: *2001: A Space Odyssey*, by Arthur C. Clarke. Have you read it?
B: No, but I saw the movie a couple of times.
A: Do you want to read it when I'm finished?
B: No, thanks. I love watching science fiction movies, but I don't like reading sci-fi books.
A: You're kidding.

Conversation 4

A: What's the matter, dear?
B: I have a terrible headache. You know I took the kids shopping for clothes today.
A: That gave you a headache?
B: We went into one of the stores that sells mostly jeans, and they were playing that rock and roll music. And it was *loud!*
A: I can't stand loud rock and roll.
B: Neither can I! Where are the aspirin?

Man: You really don't like Fellini? Or Kurosawa?
Woman: No. Not at all.
Man: How about Bergman? You must like his films.
Woman: I'm afraid not. I don't like any of his films.
Man: Oh, come on! Those men are the greats of modern cinema. I mean really...
Woman: I told you. I think they're boring. I can't stand them.
Man: Well, what movies do you like?
Woman: I like horror movies, as a matter of fact.
Man: Horror movies? You're kidding! I mean you can't be serious. Horror movies...they're so violent, so bloody, so, so, so...scary.
Woman: Well, you're obviously missing the point. You see, in horror movies you've got a classic conflict between the forces of good and the forces of evil.
Man: I just can't believe I'm hearing this. Now I suppose you'll tell me that you love heavy metal music.
Woman: No, I don't. I like classical music.
Man: You do? So do I, but I'll never watch a horror movie. You know? I also really like a good comedy, especially when I've had a hard day at the office.
Woman: Yes, I guess they're OK...but I really like a good horror movie better.

Conversation 1

Diane: Here it is...Friday night. Do you want to go dancing?
Ted: Well, not really. I'm kind of tired. I had a pretty hard week. But, how about going out to listen to some music?
Diane: What kind of music?
Ted: How about a little light jazz?
Diane: Yeah. That sounds nice.
Ted: What about the Club Blue Note?
Diane: I've never heard of it.
Ted: My office manager was there last week. He said the food and the music are terrific.
Diane: Really? What kind of food do they serve?
Ted: Mostly sandwiches and salads.
Diane: Is it expensive?
Ted: He said the prices are very good. So, do you feel like trying it?
Diane: Why not? I'll just get my coat.

Conversation 2

Oscar: Hi, Ben. What's up?
Ben: What about coming over on Sunday afternoon for a baseball party?
Oscar: A baseball party? What's that?
Ben: This Sunday's baseball game is pretty important, so I'm inviting a bunch of people from our class over to my place to watch it.
Oscar: Who's coming?
Ben: So far, there's Han, Yuki, Stefan, Anna Maria, Ricardo, Lise, and Yong.
Oscar: I'd love to, but I'm afraid I can't. My brother-in-law is coming back from Mexico City. I have to pick him up at the airport.
Ben: That's too bad. Well, how about coming over after you get back from the airport?
Oscar: OK. That's a great idea. Can I bring anything?
Ben: Whatever you like to drink. We'll order pizza for dinner.

Andrew: Hi, Barry. So, what's the plan?
Barry: Do you feel like playing tennis tonight?
Andrew: That's a good idea. I haven't played tennis in ages.
Barry: Great. Is 7:00 all right?
Andrew: Could we make it a little later? I have to work until 6:30.
Barry: That's no problem. What time do you want to meet?
Andrew: I'm sure I can make it to the tennis court by 7:30, but how about having dinner first? It's really busy around here today, and I didn't have time for lunch.
Barry: OK. I know a fantastic Mexican restaurant.
Andrew: I don't really like Mexican food. Could we go to a Chinese restaurant instead?
Barry: Yeah. The *Taste of Hong Kong* is really close to the courts.
Andrew: I've eaten there before. I liked it.
Barry: Then, why don't we meet at the restaurant?
Andrew: Sure. I'll see you there around 7:30. I'll try not to be late.

Carmen: Yoshiko, I heard that you're going back to Japan pretty soon.
Yoshiko: That's right, and boy, I am *really* busy!
Carmen: I can imagine. But listen... I'd love to get together with you before you go. Would you like to go out for dinner one night?
Yoshiko: That's a great idea. Let's see... Monday night is no good. I have to study for that final exam.
Carmen: Me, too, but I'm free on Tuesday. How about going out that night?
Yoshiko: I'm afraid I can't. I'm going out for dinner with Nancy at 6:30. Hmmm... Are you going to the last class party on Friday night? Let's go out for dinner before the party. It doesn't start until 8:00.
Carmen: I know, but it's a potluck party, so we can't go out before that. I love to eat, but I can't eat two dinners!

Yoshiko: There's always Saturday night. Are you busy then?
Carmen: No... Saturday night I'm free.
Yoshiko: I'm going to a disco with a group of friends. Do you want to join us?
Carmen: I'd really like to have a quiet dinner instead. Oh! Can I call you back? Someone's at the door.
Yoshiko: Sure. I'll be home all afternoon.

LISTEN TO THIS   UNIT 7/PAGE 51

Conversation 1

Wife: Excuse me. Could you help me?
Clerk: Certainly. What can I do for you?
Wife: We're looking for a girl's ski jacket. I like this style. Do you have it in size 10?
Clerk: Let me see...Size 4,6,8... Here we are. Size 10.
Wife: Oh. I don't really like yellow. What other colors does it come in?
Clerk: It comes in red, pink, light blue, and black.
Wife: The pink is nice. How much is it?
Clerk: It's $160.
Wife: Oh, well, we'll have to think about it.

Conversation 2

Clerk: Good afternoon. Is there something I can help you with?
Husband: Yes, there is. We'd like to see some men's leather gloves.
Clerk: Yes sir. Do you know what color or size you'd like?
Husband: What sizes do you carry?
Clerk: We carry small, medium, and large.
Husband: My son wears medium. This style is perfect. Do you have these in tan?
Clerk: I'm sorry, sir. They only come in black and brown.
Husband: Hmmm. And how much are they?
Clerk: They're usually $50, but they're on sale this week. Half price.
Husband: In that case, I think we'll take the brown.

Conversation 3

Clerk: Hi. Can I help you with something?
Wife: Yes, please. I'm interested in a golf bag for my daughter.
Clerk: Of course. I think this red and black one is very nice. It also comes in white and red, and white and navy. The quality is excellent, and it's only $150.
Wife: She's just a beginner. Do you have a smaller one?
Clerk: I'm sorry. This large size is the only size we have.
Wife: That's too bad. Well, thanks anyway.

LISTEN TO THIS   UNIT 7/PAGE 54

Conversation 1

Clerk: Yes, miss. What can I do for you today?
Customer: I'd like to return this coat and get a refund, please.
Clerk: I see. And what is the reason?
Customer: I'll show you. It's too small.
Clerk: Oh, yes. I do see. Do you have your receipt?
Customer: Here it is.

Conversation 2

Customer: Pardon me. Could you help me?
Clerk: Sure. What can I do for you?
Customer: Well, I'd like to exchange this cassette.
Clerk: What's wrong with it?
Customer: My grandson gave it to me for my birthday. It's his favorite music...but it's too noisy for me. I want something quieter.
Clerk: I'm really sorry, but there are no exchanges on tapes after they've been opened.

Conversation 3

Clerk: Good morning, sir. What can I help you with today?
Customer: I'd like to exchange this sweater, please. I just bought it about half an hour ago. I have my receipt right here in the bag.
Clerk: What's the problem?
Customer: I decided that I don't really like the color. I think I like the orange one better.
Clerk: You're right. The orange one would look better than the brown one. I'll just switch them for you.

PERSON TO PERSON   UNIT 7/PAGES 55-56

Joan: This is a really good store. I bet you can find everything you need for Europe right here.
Kerry: I hope so. I have a lot to do before the trip.
Joan: Do you know what you need?
Kerry: Not too much, really. Pants, a light jacket, and a sweater.
Joan: Here are the pants. Oh! This is a nice pair. They're black, so they'll go with everything.
Kerry: Except, if it's sunny, they'll be too hot. Besides, I already have black ones at home. How about these pink pants?
Joan: They're a much nicer color.
Kerry: And they feel like a better quality, too. I'll try them on later. Let's look for a sweater now.... I like this purple one.
Joan: Do you? I really think it's too plain. What do you think of this white one? It's fancier, so you could wear it in the evening.
Kerry: I know, but the purple one is looser. It'll be more comfortable.
Anyway, I have some fancy sweaters at home.
Joan: Well, try the purple, then.
Kerry: Let's see, I guess the last thing is the jacket.
Joan: Look at this beige suede jacket. It's beautiful, but I know it's too heavy for the summer.
Kerry: It's also too expensive! I don't want to spend that much money. Do you see any cotton jackets?
Joan: Right over here. Oh, these are much lighter.
Kerry: And a lot more useful!

LISTEN TO THIS   UNIT 8/PAGE 59

Cashier: Hi. Is everybody ready to order?
Father: Yes, I think so. Davey? What are you going to have?
Davey: I want a cheeseburger, large french fries, and a chocolate milk shake.
Father: Davey...are you sure you can eat all that?

Davey: Sure, Dad! I'm starving!
Father: OK. How about you dear? What are you having?
Mother: I haven't decided yet. You go ahead.
Father: OK. I'll have the chicken nuggets, a large order of fries, and a coffee.
Cashier: What kind of sauce do you want for the chicken nuggets?
Father: Let's see...You have sweet and sour sauce and honey sauce...I'll take the sweet and sour sauce.
Mother: OK, well then... I think I'll have the fish sandwich, a garden salad, and a coffee.
Cashier: And what kind of dressing for your salad?
Mother: Oh, ummm. French dressing, please.
Cashier: All right. So... the little boy is having a cheeseburger, large fries, and a chocolate milk shake. You're having chicken nuggets with sweet and sour sauce, large fries and a coffee, and your wife is having a fish sandwich, a garden salad with French dressing, and a coffee.
Father: That's right.
Cashier: Is that for here or to go?

LISTEN TO THIS UNIT 8/PAGE 62

Conversation 1
Waitress: Would you like something to drink?
Woman: Do you have apple juice?
Waitress: No, I'm sorry. We have orange, tomato, and cranberry.
Woman: OK. I'll take orange. A large one, please.

Conversation 2
Waitress: Would you care for some dessert?
Man: Well... What do you have?
Waitress: Tonight we have cheesecake, homemade pie, sherbet, and a fresh fruit salad with whipped cream.
Man: Do you have any ice cream?
Waitress: Yes, sir. We have vanilla, chocolate, and maple walnut.
Man: What kind of pie do you have?
Waitress: Pecan, peach, and apple.
Man: Could I have pecan pie with some vanilla ice cream on the side?
Waitress: Certainly, sir.

Conversation 3
Waiter: Shall I bring you some more coffee?
Woman: Please. I'd love some.
Waiter: Here you are, ma'am.
Woman: And could I get a little more cream, please?
Waiter: Of course. Anything else?
Woman: I think...just the check, thanks.
Waiter: Right away.

PERSON TO PERSON UNIT 8/PAGES 63–64

Waiter: Have you decided yet, sir?
Man: Yes, I think so. Marian?
Woman: Yes, I'll have the salmon teriyaki, please.
Waiter: And what kind of potatoes would you like with that?

Woman: Baked, please. For the vegetable, I'd like broccoli.
Waiter: And would you care for soup or salad to start?
Man: What is your soup today?
Waiter: We have cream of cauliflower and French onion.
Woman: Oh, they both sound heavy. I think I'll have a salad, please.
Waiter: Very good. With what kind of dressing?
Woman: I'd like blue cheese. Oh, wait, could you change that to oil and vinegar?
Waiter: Certainly. And you, sir? What will you have?
Man: Those lobster tails look pretty good.
Waiter: I'm very sorry, sir. We don't have any lobster tonight.
Man: No lobster? Well... I guess I'll take the steak then. Could you tell the chef I like my steak very rare?
Waiter: Of course. Mashed, boiled, or baked potatoes?
Man: Mashed, please.
Waiter: Vegetable?
Man: I'd like asparagus.
Waiter: And, soup or salad?
Man: I think I'm going to try the cream of cauliflower. I've never had that before.
Waiter: Dessert?
Woman: We'll decide later, if that's all right. But, could you bring me some extra butter with my potato?
Waiter: Certainly. Anything to drink while you wait?
Woman: An iced coffee, please.
Man: Make that two.

LISTEN TO THIS UNIT 9/PAGE 67

Conversation 1
Woman: Oh no! The machine says, "Use correct change only." All I have is quarters.
Man: Don't worry. I have lots of change.
Woman: Do you have an extra dime?
Man: Sure. Here you go.

Conversation 2
Woman: OK... books, tape recorder, tapes, purse...let's see... yeah ...that's everything.
Boy: Can I carry something for you?
Woman: No. That's OK. I've got it all. But...could you please get the door and the lights for me?
Boy: Of course!

Conversation 3
Brother: Oh, wow. I'm exhausted!
Sister: Why?
Brother: I stayed up until 3:00 AM studying for that exam today. I was up at 7:00, at school by a quarter to nine...We took the exam from 9:00 to 11:30. Then we had basketball practice from 1:00 to 3:00.
Sister: That's a lot.
Brother: Yeah... Could you do the dishes tonight? I know it's my turn, but I'm just too tired.
Sister: Sure. You can do them for me tomorrow night.
Brother: It's a deal...and thanks. I appreciate it.

Conversation 4

Woman: Have you seen the rain? It's pouring out there!

Man: No, really? I have to walk to the bank on my lunch hour.

Woman: Did you remember your umbrella this morning?

Man: No. I forgot it. If you're not going outside at lunch, could I please borrow yours?

Woman: I'm sorry. I didn't bring mine today, either.

Conversation 5

Marge: Hi, Atsuko. How're you?

Atsuko: Great, Marge. What's new? Would you like to come in for coffee?

Marge: I'd love to, but to tell you the truth, I'm right in the middle of making Rachel's birthday cake, and I'm out of eggs. Do you think I could borrow a couple?

Atsuko: Oh, sure. No problem. How many do you need?

Marge: Just two.

Atsuko: Wait a minute. I'll get them.

Conversation 6

Woman: Oh... there they are. Of course they're on the top shelf. It's no use. Tsk!...Oh. Excuse me. Excuse me!

Clerk: Yes, ma'am. What can I do for you?

Woman: Hi. Sorry to bother you. Could you do me a favor? I need one of those jars of pickles on the top shelf, but I can't reach it. Could you please get it down for me?

Clerk: Sure. Here you go.

LISTEN TO THIS   UNIT 9/PAGE 70

Conversation 1

A: Excuse me!

B: Yes, ma'am? What can I do for you?

A: I have a problem with this coffee maker, and I want my money back.

B: Well, what seems to be the problem?

A: The problem is that it doesn't work! I've only used it three times.

B: I'd be happy to exchange it for you.

A: Thank you, but I'd like a refund, please. I invited six people to my place for dinner last night. After dinner, I plugged in the coffee maker, I put in the coffee and water, I turned it on, and nothing happened! I was very embarrassed. Now, I'd like my money back.

B: Of course. Here's your refund. And I'm really very sorry about all this.

A: That's OK. And thank you for your help.

Conversation 2

A: Next, please!

B: Yes, I just received my telephone bill, and there's a problem with it.

A: And what exactly is the problem?

B: There's a collect call from Finland on there, and I don't know anyone in Finland! I'm very upset. Could you please take the charge off my bill?

A: May I see your bill, please?

B: Certainly. There it is. On July 1st. I really don't know anybody in Finland.

A: OK, don't worry. I'll take the call off. Let's see... it was $42. Your bill was $66.10, minus $42, so your new total is $24.10. I'm very sorry about the mistake.

B: That's OK. It wasn't your fault.

LISTEN TO THIS   UNIT 10/PAGE 75

Paula: That's enough about me. How about you? Are you from Los Angeles?

Brad: No. Actually, I was born in Seattle, but I guess you could say I grew up all over the world.

Paula: Huh? What do you mean?

Brad: Well, my dad was in the Air Force, so we moved around a lot, starting when I was two. That was when we moved to Japan...just outside Tokyo.

Paula: Wow. Did you go to school there?

Brad: No. My father was sent to Germany after that. We moved to Munich in 1960, when I was five. I started elementary school there.

Paula: Where did you go after that?

Brad: Well! After Munich we lived in the Middle East, we moved there when I was ten, then Germany again, Alaska, and then Hawaii. In 1972 my father retired. Was it 1972? Yes...because I was seventeen.

Paula: Did you come to Los Angeles then?

Brad: No. My dad decided to retire in Hawaii. I really liked it there, so I went to the University of Hawaii.

Paula: So when did you come to Los Angeles?

Brad: Right after I finished college. I really feel like L.A. is my home now.

LISTEN TO THIS   UNIT 10/PAGE 78

When we think about Hemingway the writer, we also have to think about Hemingway, the man. In many ways, his life was as interesting as his work. Like many great authors, many of his books and stories were based on his personal experiences. Let's look at some of these books and see how his experiences influenced them.

In 1925, he published his first collection of short stories, called *In Our Time*. Most of the stories were really about his childhood. A year later, in 1926, his first two novels appeared — *Torrents of Spring*, and *The Sun Also Rises*. Remember, Hemingway lived in Paris during the early twenties. When he lived there, he knew many famous writers and artists. *The Sun Also Rises* is about some of those talented, but lonely and angry people.

Hemingway drove an ambulance during World War I — that was between 1914 and 1918. Many years later, in 1929, he used this experience when he wrote his fourth novel, *A Farewell to Arms*. This book, which was a love story about an American ambulance driver and a British nurse, made him famous throughout the world.

After that, during the 1930s, Hemingway continued to write short stories and also wrote two books about subjects he greatly loved. *Death in the Afternoon* was about bullfighting, and *The Green Hills of Africa* was about big game hunting. His father, a doctor, got him interested in hunting, fishing, sports, and the outdoor life when he was a child.

When the Second World War began, Hemingway returned to Europe. This time he was there as a reporter, so he was present at many of the most important battles of the war. He used these war experiences to write *Across the River and Into the Trees*. This book was not very successful, and people thought he was losing his magic.

But, in 1952, he wrote a short novel, *The Old Man and the Sea*. For this book, he won the Pulitzer Prize. And two years later, he received the Nobel Prize for Literature. The book tells the story of an old Cuban fisherman, but is really about man against nature. Why is it his best? As I said, when he was younger, he used to go fishing with his father, and in later years, deep-sea fishing remained his favorite hobby. He was able to write a powerful, emotional story because of his own personal experiences.

Sadly in 1961, sick and unable to live the active life he loved and wrote about, Hemingway killed himself with one of his own shotguns.

LISTEN TO THIS   UNIT 11/PAGE 83

Lin: Minako! How was your trip? I'm dying to hear all about it.
Minako: It was fantastic, Lin. I loved it.
Lin: So, what did you think of San Francisco?
Minako: Beautiful. Have you ever been there?
Lin: No, I haven't, but I've always wanted to go. So...convince me. Tell me all about it.
Minako: Hmmm. Where do I start? It really is a wonderful city. Mostly because it's so different, I think. Everywhere you look there are hilly streets, beautiful old Victorian homes and buildings, the bay, and of course the Golden Gate Bridge.
Lin: Was it easy to get around?
Minako: Oh, yeah. I walked a lot, but when I got tired it was easy to get a bus. The bus system is really efficient and inexpensive, but the buses are a bit run-down. I also took the subway a couple of times. It was cheap, fast, and comfortable.
Lin: How about the cable cars?
Minako: They were always packed with people, but they were really fun to ride.
Lin: What are the restaurants like?
Minako: There's a real variety. We had seafood at the Fisherman's Wharf. It was really fresh and delicious, but it was kind of expensive. And we went to Chinatown for dinner one night. The food there was really spicy, but good.
Lin: How was your hotel?
Minako: It was small and very old. I felt like I was in an old movie! It wasn't fancy at all, but it was clean and well-kept, and the rates were quite reasonable.
Lin: Sounds wonderful. San Francisco, here I come.

LISTEN TO THIS   UNIT 11/PAGE 86

Susan: Excuse me, Elaine, do you know any hotels in Boston? The boss is sending me there, and I have to find a place to stay.
Elaine: I know three... There's The Midtown, The Boston Bay, and The Fairfield.
Susan: What are the locations like? I'll be downtown most of the time.
Elaine: The Midtown has the best location, then. The Boston Bay is also good, but the Fairfield isn't downtown at all.
Susan: I've read about the The Boston Bay. It's also the newest hotel in Boston, isn't it?
Elaine: Yeah, I think so. It's the biggest, and it has a very good restaurant. But, I think it's the most expensive hotel in Boston.
Susan: I have to keep my expenses down. What about The Midtown?
Elaine: I have a hotel guidebook here someplace. Let me check. Here we are... The Midtown is cheaper than the Boston Bay. Oh, but it doesn't have a restaurant.
Susan: Could you look up The Fairfield?
Elaine: Sure. The room rates are the cheapest, probably because it's not downtown. My parents stayed at The Fairfield last year. It's a really nice, old hotel. They ate in the restaurant there. It's one of the best in Boston.
Susan: OK... Well, the Midtown sounds best. Could you reserve a room for me there?
Elaine: Sure. What days will you be there?

PERSON TO PERSON   UNIT 11/PAGES 87–88

Bob: Well, Ruth. It was great to get away, but it's good to be home again.
Ruth: It really was a wonderful trip. So, which city did you like best, Paris, London, or Rome?
Bob: That's hard to say. There were good things and bad things about all three cities.
Ruth: Wait a minute! What bad things?
Bob: Traffic, for one. The traffic in London was pretty bad, and the traffic in Paris was even worse! I was afraid to cross the street.
Ruth: That's true...and how about Rome? I thought Rome was worse than Paris. Those drivers are crazy! And always honking their horns! It was really noisy there.
Bob: Paris was noisy, too. A lot noisier than it was in London.
Ruth: You're right, but I still think Rome was noisier than Paris!
Bob: Well, all big cities have bad traffic and a lot of noise. Let's not think about the bad things. Think about all those art galleries we visited.
Ruth: Yeah, the art galleries in Rome were fantastic, but I thought the Paris art galleries were better. Of course, I've always dreamed of going to the Louvre.
Bob: Me, too. I loved the galleries in London, but I liked the ones in Paris even more. The restaurants in Paris were better than in London, too. I thought the food was more interesting. It had more flavor.
Ruth: And the food in Rome was incredible! I liked the Italian restaurants better than the French ones. I thought they were more interesting. Before we went to Rome, I thought Italian food was all pizza and spaghetti!
Bob: Really! I'm sure I put on weight in Rome.

Ruth: Maybe not. We did a lot of dancing at night. Those discos in Rome were great, but I think I liked the Paris nightlife better. It was more romantic.

Bob: You know where I had more fun in the evening? In London. Paris was good, but I thought the London nightlife was better.

Ruth: Yeah, we saw a couple of great plays. Oh, I'll never decide which city I liked best.

Bob: Me, neither.

LISTEN TO THIS   UNIT 12/PAGE 91

Jim: Good morning, Ms. Reynolds. I have your schedule for Monday of next week.

Irene: Thanks, Jim. Am I going to have any free time?

Jim: A little, but it's going to be a pretty busy day.

Irene: OK. Let's start with the morning.

Jim: All right. From 8:00 to 10:00 you're going to have breakfast with the vice presidents. Then you'll drive to the new factory. After you get there, around 10:30, there will be a tour of the new building.

Irene: How long is that going to take?

Jim: About an hour.

Irene: And after that?

Jim: At one o'clock, the managers from Chicago and New York will be here for the monthly meeting.

Irene: OK.

Jim: At seven o'clock, you're going to go to the TV station for an interview with a TV newswoman. Just a few questions about the new factory.

Irene: Anything else?

Jim: Just one more thing. The Business Club dinner.

Irene: Oh, right. And I've already written my speech for that.

Jim: So, you'll get there around 8:00. They're planning to serve dinner around 8:30, and you're going to give your speech at 9:30. The dinner meeting will end at eleven. By the way, I'm sure the food will be delicious.

Irene: Hmm. I'll go on a diet on Tuesday. And thanks for all your work, Jim.

Jim: My pleasure.

LISTEN TO THIS   UNIT 12/PAGE 94

Max: I can't believe it! The last day of school is finally here. What are you going to do this summer, Alessandro?

Alessandro: Well, starting tomorrow, I'm going to work in my Dad's restaurant.

Max: Really? Starting tomorrow? So soon?

Alessandro: I really want to save some extra money for college.

Max: Are you taking any time off?

Alessandro: Yeah. I'm not going to work weekends, and I'm going away the last three weeks of the summer.

Max: What are you going to do on the weekends? Just take it easy?

Alessandro: I don't know...maybe read a few books or rent some movies. Whatever.

Max: Sounds kind of boring.

Alessandro: Not really. I'm going to go to a friend's cabin by the lake most weekends. I want to do a little waterskiing and swimming. Let's hope for good weather!

Max: Now that sounds like fun!

Alessandro: Yeah. I'm looking forward to it. My friend and his dad are building a new dock this summer, and I'd really like to help them.

Max: How about the last three weeks? Are you going somewhere special?

Alessandro: I'm going to Italy to visit my uncle for two weeks. He lives in Rome. I'm also going to do a bit of traveling with my cousin while I'm there.

Max: What cities are you going to visit?

Alessandro: I've never been to Italy, so my cousin is deciding. We might go to Milan, we might go to Venice, or we might go to Florence. I'm not sure yet.

Max: And what are you doing the last week?

Alessandro: I'm moving to an apartment near the college, so I hope to get everything organized before school starts.

PERSON TO PERSON   UNIT 12/PAGES 95–96

Ben: You know what, Jill? You work too hard. Let's go and sit in the park.

Jill: I can't do that. I have to study. Final exams are next week.

Ben: But, Jill...You already know that you're going to go to Harvard! What are you going to major in, anyway?

Jill: I'm taking Business and Economics. How about you? Which school are you going to next year, Ben?

Ben: Actually, I'm going to work for my dad for a year. I'll go to college the year after that.

Jill: What do you want to study?

Ben: I'm not really sure. I'd like to study literature or art. So, do you want to work for a big company after college, or do you want to have your own business?

Jill: Neither. I hope to get into law school after I finish at Harvard.

Ben: Wow. You sure are ambitious!

Jill: What kind of job do you want to have after college?

Ben: Something easy. I'd like to work nine to five. I guess you'll be a lawyer.

Jill: Uh-huh. I'd like to practice law for a few years, and then I hope to go into politics.

Ben: Well, I just hope to have a steady job and a nice family.

Jill: Really? I want to make a lot of money.

Ben: Anything else?

Jill: Sure... I'd like to be president someday!